Elsie's Mountain

Memoirs compiled by
Barbara Anne Waite

Memories of Palomar
& Southern California
1897-1987

Elsie's Mountain: Memories of Palomar & Southern California 1897-1987
Library of Congress Control Number: 2015914437
ISBN: 978-0-9839452-1-5

Cover and text design by Diane King, dkingdesigner.com

Published by Palomar Mountain Bookworks
        2382 Primrose Ave., Vista, CA 92083

BarbaraAnneWaite.com

Printed in the United States of America.

Contents

Los Angeles

• Pomona

• Riverside

• Corona

Long Beach
•

*Alternate
Routes to
Palomar*

Santa

• Temescal

Terminal Island

• Elsinore

El Toro

Ana

San Juan
Capistrano

Mtns

• Temecula

Santa Catalina Island

Santa
Margarita
Rancho

• Pala

• Palomar

• Mission San Luis Rey

• Escondido

• Ramona

25 Miles

La Mesa

San Diego   •

Tijuana, Mexico

4

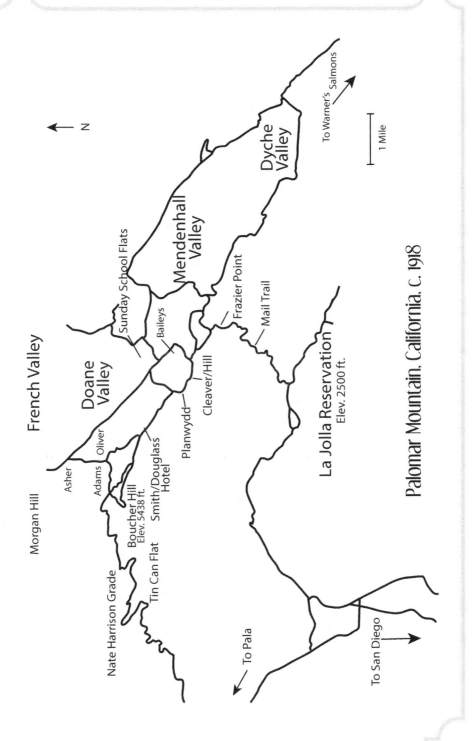

Palomar Mountain, California, c. 1918

Author's Notes

It was an innocent and simple venture—my mother had saved my Grandma Elsie's diaries and I glanced through them after her death. Interest in that bygone era absorbed me as I poured over those pages and handled her mementos. It seemed as though I were viewing a sweet Hallmark-style, vintage movie as I learned of Elsie's tragic Arizona love before she met my grandfather. Unearthing even more family history, I began to transcribe her diary and letters. Clearly, her vast collection of memories and history as she lived it needed to be shared.

Elsie was a master storyteller. I had the privilege of knowing my grandmother for almost forty years, and what I remember best was her ability to recall and depict events from her childhood as if they happened that day. My first book, *Elsie: Adventures of an Arizona School Teacher 1913–1916*, recounted her vivid recollections of life as a "mail-order" teacher in the "untamed west."

There were no plans for a second book. Yet, as a family project, I transcribed the years from her diary that recorded the birth of my mother and the time between 1918 and 1924. She had saved many wonderful photographs from Palomar. It was interpretive history—especially interesting, but it did not make a book. Then one day, searching through an old cedar chest, my sister Nancy and I came across letters disclosing stories we had never heard.

Neither Elsie nor my mother had spoken much about The Great Depression or World War II. My grandfather Jack died eight months before I was born, and Elsie did not talk about him a great deal, except to tell of the years spent on Palomar and the apple ranch. I began to survey the letters and slowly discovered a further story, one Elsie never related. An Elsie I had never imagined became unveiled, and my respect for this precious, gentle woman deepened.

We come from a long line of "keepers of history." I wouldn't say we're hoarders—I'd rather say we are one with old letters and documents and nuggets of the past. Our discovery of the letters piqued my interest in determining more about my grandmother's life. I found a heavy box filled with manuscripts and poems among my grandmother's keepsakes. In it were records of when she sold her stories and for how much. A large file of newspaper articles about Palomar, several of them mentioning Jack or Elsie, was included in the find. Also among her treasures was a tattered post-Civil War news article recounting how her father, Alonzo, as a child, had been wounded during the war.

My search revealed the pages torn from Elsie's journal describing the train ride from Virginia to California in 1897. Over the years, she had scribbled notes on scraps of paper, old envelopes, and on the backs of discarded mail. I felt like a private detective as I searched through stacks of yellowing papers. And like a private detective, I uncovered answers to my growing list of questions. Even such odd pieces of information as census records and war bonds disclosed surprises. Outside research helped fill in details, such as the fact Elsie's physical symptoms in 1918 (malaise, hair loss) indicated, as she suspected, that she most likely had the Spanish Influenza, which killed more than 50 million people worldwide in a year.

Much of Elsie's narrative in this book comes straight from the pages she compiled in her old age. She penned notes about Virginia, her college days, and much about the apple ranch and resort and the workers they hired. Her notes about mountain characters easily became her narrative. I was thankful for the day-to-day records written by Robert Asher and edited by Peter Brueggeman, as they also helped me recreate mountain life.

I left most of it as she composed it. Elsie's story took place in a rapidly changing America. Unfortunately, it was an America still steeped in strong racial and social divides. Some of the vocabulary Elsie and others used reflected the common views of the time. I have kept them to retain authenticity, although I do not agree with their use, and I am glad such words and views are neither acceptable nor common today.

Elsie's writing comes laced with old-fashioned terms. Few today would write of going on a "tramp," or "tinting" a cottage, or attending "normal school" (Teacher Training College). My computer software suggested changes to some of her outmoded expressions. However, I bypassed its advice and chose to retain the flavor of Elsie's own description of events. Fewer and fewer people in our modern culture experience her world of writing real letters (with pen and paper), or reading aloud with their family. Taking part in the "war effort" or going "calling" are not a part of our everyday language today. Elsie lived at a time when women spent weeks in bed because of a miscarriage or birthing of a baby.

Few today keep journals. Some write blogs. But day-to-day accounts or ordinary simple events go unrecorded, if not unnoticed. I am thankful I recorded on cassette tape her stories, her chuckle, and her zest for life. I am grateful my mother saved all of Elsie's boxes, for their contents hold vast records of a bygone life.

There is value in viewing the past, the ordinary, if it causes us to pause and examine the present. Elsie never seemed too busy to notice the first flowers of spring (often found peeking through the snow-dusted earth), to slow her pace, read, and sometimes move her bed outside to view the stars, experience the wind, the night sounds, and the earthy mountain smells. The letters also unveiled her gift of offering grace to her loved ones. Perhaps Elsie's story will encourage us to stop, see the beauty everywhere, and develop grace to those with whom we live.

I have tried not to interpret Elsie's story. In the book by Markus Zusak, *The Book Thief*, Max says to Liesel when giving her a blank notebook, "Words are life, Liesel. All those pages, they're for you to fill. I'm not lost to you, Liesel. You will always be able to find me in your words. That's where I'll live on." Elsie's words live on to tell her story.

Elsie's Mountain lives on in the notebooks she filled with words. My hope is that you find her here in the book, in her own words and on her own mountain.

Introduction

This is my last story. Stories have always been a great source of joy for me. A long lifetime I have lived with my senses expectant, my attention focused, never wanting to miss any part of God's beautiful creation. I have seen and loved much. My heart's wellspring of words overflows to the page, no longer captive by my mind.

Words. I love them. They fill my mind and spill over onto the paper. It was my love of reading from an early age that sparked this love of words, in fairy tales and daring adventure stories—my favorites. Fueled by these tales, my imagination took flight and poured out stories and poetry of my own from the tender age of nine. I continued this pursuit for the rest of my life. My own childhood experiences inspired many of my stories sold to children's magazines over the years.

Ah, the rush of memory that comes on the wings of a familiar aroma. My daughter Catherine came by this morning bearing a basket full of fragrant apples, Palomar Mountain apples picked from apple trees planted by my Papa over eighty years ago. I am flooded with cherished memories of little Catherine tucked safely inside an apple box beneath those trees, content as I tend the orchard.

Tucked in with the apples Catherine brought was a little surprise. Nestled there was a newspaper article that referred to me, written by my friend, Larry Littlefield. He had written, "Elsie has a mind as sharp as an Ansel Adams photograph." Oh my, such a generous compliment. I consider myself very fortunate for such a description at ninety-seven.

From the moment I arrived on Palomar Mountain in 1904, I claimed it as my own right then and there. My feet sent down roots into the earth. Though I would live too many years apart from this place I loved, my devotion and longing were always for my "mountain." My fondest memories still linger, filled with fresh mountain air and birds' songs echoing through the treetops.

They wash over me and I am young again, renewed. These days I need a walker to get around, but my memories are a liberator—entertaining, amusing and encouraging.

I will begin my story in Virginia where my life began—lush, green, beautiful Virginia. When we arrived in California, I missed the verdant landscape we left behind. Not until we discovered Palomar Mountain did I feel, at last, my heart had found her home.

Catherine has long encouraged me to compile my memories of the mountain. Over the years, I have written morsels and scraps, kept journals of my time there, and now I shall begin. Reading once again my old journals and letters induces reflection. Words penned years ago have faded, some blurred by teardrops of joy or sorrow. As my story unfolds, I sometimes find it necessary to knit both past and present together, as memories become fainter. For those who love history and creation's high places, I share with you my mountain memories.

—Elsie Roberts

1

My Virginia Childhood

Thoughts of a Child
Elsie Reed Hayes (1904)

Strange seems the heart of man
Unto a little child,
Who understandeth not
Even her own quaint thoughts
Why in the depths of woods
She thrills with wondrous joy
Why, when the thunder rolls,
She finds in awe delight.
Why, when the clouds are dark
She sorrows secretly
Under the countless stars,
Hearing sweet music,
Why she kneels, worshipping.

The Pentagon is now on or very near the site of my family home—the very house where I was born. The area now called Arlington they then called Ballston—earlier Balls Crossroads, later Clarendon. It was in this house on January 22, 1888, that I was born, in the same year that Virginia would celebrate its 100th birthday as a state.

It delights me to think that my early roots connected closely to significant historical sites near our nation's capital.

My mother, May Carrie Reed, before her marriage lived in a nearby village close to the National Cemetery and General Lee's old home. She worked as a young schoolteacher and my Papa, like most young suitors of the day, "courted" her by coming to call at her home. Moreover, like most fathers, William Narin Reed would sit in the parlor and oversee the two young people.

My parents told how Grandma Reed would make her thoughts known. "Pa they don't want you there!" she would say.

Grandpa Reed had his own ideas. "When the right man comes along, I'll leave the room."

When my father, Alonzo Hayes, came to call on the pretty girl who became my mother, Grandpa Reed would sit and chat with his daughter and Alonzo for only a few minutes. Then he would leave the room. My mother then knew that Alonzo had met the approval to be her suitor. He could not object to Alonzo being nearly ten years older than May, for William Reed himself had been thirty-three years older than his second wife Amelia, May's stepmother. At that time, he had three children who were older than his new wife!

Grandpa Reed and his brother Philip went west to seek their fortunes in 1849. He first took his wife Hylinda and five children (the oldest child nine and the youngest, my mother May, a year old) to her parents in New York. As captain of a caravan of forty-niners, he ventured out across the wild untamed country to reach California, the land of gold. Hardships filled the journey. At one point, he climbed a hill to see if there were any signs of the trail ahead and to look for hostile Indians. Suddenly, Indians surrounded him—their bowstrings drawn and ready at a moment's notice to let their arrows fly. Grandpa

Reed, known for his hearty laugh, now in the face of certain death and with no possibility of escape apparent, threw back his head and laughed loud and long. The Indians evidently thought that no one who would laugh at death could be merely a man, but a god. They slipped away silently.

When Grandpa Reed left San Francisco, he sailed down to the Isthmus of Panama (no canal then), walked across the narrow thirty-mile-wide strip, and boarded a ship back to New York.

Only nine years old when her mother died, my mother, the youngest of nine children by Hylinda and William, went to live with an older sister Alice Reed Howdle. Two years later her father, fifty-eight years old, married Amelia Hanford, age twenty-five. May lived with them, as eventually did her three younger half-sisters: Florence, Ella, and Minnie. She thus felt comfortable in a full household when she married my father, even when they lived in his childhood home with his mother and two unmarried sisters.

Papa, Alonzo Gilman Hayes, had been born in Massachusetts. The Hayes relatives immigrated to America in 1680. Ephraim Gilman, Papa's grandfather, owned ships and imported goods from distant places. Papa's mother, Amanda Malvina Gilman, came from Alexandria near where George Washington attended church. Not far away, Mount Vernon stood on the banks of the Potomac River.

Papa's father, a Congregational minister in Barnstable, Massachusetts, became ill while serving there. Probably due to my Grandfather Hayes' poor health, the family moved to Virginia. My grandfather died at age forty-eight. That left my widowed grandmother Amanda Gilman Hayes with four children: Annie, Mary, Alonzo, and Douglas. Amanda stayed on with her children in the house that became my birthplace. Our home was only two or three miles from the White House, but because it was across the Potomac River, it necessitated quite a trip by horse and buggy to reach the nation's capital.

The Civil War erupted while Papa's family lived in that home. My grandmother's Washington family, the Gilmans, begged her to come with her fatherless children to be with them, but she refused. When Confederate troops came quite near, rumors circulated of the troops burning homes as they approached. Then she did stay with them overnight, but only one time, and only then because of the frightening reports.

I knew Grandmother Hayes as "Grammie." One of my earliest memories is of my older sister Hylinda and me sitting on the kitchen floor, one of us on each side of Grammie while she fed us from a bowl of bread milk. Each in turn, she gave us a spoonful. "This little bird, then, this little bird," she said.

My life in Virginia had the essence of a fairytale. Our home perched on a charming hilltop among old oaks looking down into a green valley. The clear stream running through the valley evidently curved because I remember how we children used to run down from behind the house to where the strong branches of a tree hung over the water. My thoughtful father cut through a heavy branch so that it hung free. Strongly entangled overhead, it made a safer swing than if hand-tied and knotted above us.

What marvelous fun to catch hold of the free branch and swing out over the water. The huge box that had crated the new piano, Papa placed where we could climb upon it and so swing higher and farther out over the brook. Our life in Virginia seemed like child heaven to us.

My cousin Janet and I made mud pies—lemon ones—because we could color them with yellow wildflowers. I ate it for verisimilitude and shocked mother's stepmother, Grandma Reed. As to eating mud, mother said when I was a baby I licked sand when Aunt Mamie took Hylinda and me to visit Uncle Board at the Atlantic Ocean. A woman at the beach spoke to my mother agitatedly, "Lady, your little girl is eating sand!" Uncle Board, a noted doctor, said it would not hurt me, and I must have something in my system that required it.

Janet and I also built playhouses in the woods by twining branches together. I cannot imagine a child in a more ideal situation. We thrived with devoted parents, sisters and a brother and cousins. We even had two aunts we imagined were like extra parents. With a fascinating city nearby, and the brook and woods for Aunt Annie to take me for early spring walks, I had a delightful childhood. My aunt showed me where to find

Top Left—Virginia hired maid; Top right—Hylinda and Elsie;
Bottom—Virginia home—Sunny Bank in Ballston with Hayes family, May's
mother and Alonzo's sisters

trailing arbutus, pansies and anemones, and thus began my knowledge and love for plants that would remain with me the rest of my life.

I never heard an unkind word in our home. I only remember being spanked one time. Sent to the store and told to come right back, I failed to obey. Along the way I passed one of the hired girls, a wonderful storyteller, and I sat and listened to a story instead.

We used to drive to Arlington to see my mother's stepmother, Grandma Amelia Hanford Reed. Very old and deaf, she used an ear trumpet, a contrivance used to magnify the sound. It embarrassed me as a small child to speak into it, but I did love to slide down the horsehair back of her sofa, though it felt tickly.

We visited Fort Myers, near Arlington, to see the stunts performed by the magnificent horses of the cavalry unit there. When the Barnum and Bailey Circus came to Washington, Papa took us into the city to see it. The acrobats particularly thrilled me, so I had a new ambition. I wanted to be an acrobat.

An old part of the house, a cozy, comfortable room called the snuggery was my favorite room. An old back stairs led up to the little room for the hired girl, just across the hall from the dining room and kitchen. The front-hall stairs led up to the bedrooms above, heated in winter by a vent from the room below. Hylinda and I slept in the bedroom across from Mama and Papa.

Perhaps any kind of indoor bathroom in country homes around us seemed a novelty, but our bathroom I remember as particularly special. There was some kind of tub, probably a forerunner of today's bathtubs. Of course, we still also had an outside privy.

The aunts added a new wing with long porches upstairs and down, a wide hall that gave entrance to a dining room and a gracious staircase that led up to their bedrooms. Downstairs included the front parlor with its glass-fronted bookcases. I practiced piano in that room and pored over the treasures in the fine bookcase.

I have happy vivid memories of hearing my name called from above as I played in the front yard. Aunt Mamie appeared, leaning over the banister of the upper porch. Knowing what this meant, I

Top—Mary Hayes with her Sunday School class in Virginia that included Charles Munson and Anna and Tom DeLashmutt (nephews and niece of Alonzo) circa 1890; Bottom—Invitation Church Society at Sunny Bank; Left—Aunt Annie Hayes

You are cordially invited to attend

+A GARDEN PARTY+

UNDER THE AUSPICES OF THE

Church Improvement Society,

AT SUNNY BANK.

THE HOME OF MRS. HAYES,

For the Benefit of the Presbyterian Church, at Balston, Virginia.

On Thursday Evening, August 16.

(IF RAINY THE FOLLOWING DAY.)

Supper and Refreshments Served by the Ladies of the Church.

Stages leave the car stand in Georgetown from 5 to 8.30 p. m. for the grounds, returning in time for cars.

would run and stand under it. "Hold up your pinafore!" Aunt Mamie called down.

Sweets "from the sky" dropped into my pinafore in the form of little packets of candy. How inexpressibly fascinating having sweets dropped from above seemed to me as a child!

Aunt Cornelia told us Aunt Mamie had forty beaus. A petite woman, "As small as the Lord ever made a perfect woman," Aunt Mamie used to say with a twinkle in her eye. "If they are any smaller than I am, they're pygmies and dwarfs." In a teenage picture of her in hoop skirt and with rows of curls, she appeared bewitching indeed— and remained cute and charming even into old age.

Aunt Annie encouraged my reading—though because I loved reading, this extra motivation remained unnecessary. I well remember Aunt Annie reading *Alice in Wonderland*. Aunt Mamie laughed so hard that Aunt Annie had to stop. In turn, Papa always used to have to pause now and then to wipe his eyes when he read Dickens, moved to tears, the pathos or humor causing him to laugh until he cried. Aunt Annie also encouraged my writing as a very young child. I loved composing little stories and verses in childish script.

Each grown-up had particular claim on a certain child. Papa naturally had Gilman, the only boy. Mama had the youngest child, Alice, and Aunt Mamie sponsored Hylinda. Aunt Annie claimed me, and therefore influenced me tremendously.

My two spinster aunts were remarkable women. Aunt Annie, considered the first woman to hold an important post with the government, always had an efficient and businesslike manner. Annie (then only nineteen years old) went to work in Washington in 1863, after her father's death. She did this in spite of the fact that the Civil War raged nearby. She advanced in the Bureau of Engraving and Printing until she became Superintendent of Orders. Aunt Annie showed President Rutherford B. Hayes around the Bureau when he came to inspect it. In their chat about their mutual surname, they came to the realization that they were distant cousins.

Aunt Annie had a little autograph album that she took to Congress. She obtained signatures from Abraham Lincoln and several other men who were then members of Congress and later became presidents of the United States. Annie performed so many unheralded deeds of kindness that at her death the Bureau department head said of her, "If she had been a Catholic, she would've been made a saint."

Aunt Annie's devoted sister, Aunt Mamie, demonstrated a different type of success. She was essentially domestic, a homebody who kept house for herself and Aunt Annie for many years. Aunt Mamie remained decidedly feminine and old fashioned, while Aunt Annie demonstrated efficiency and accomplishment. Each of our aunts had her own quaint and charming ways, and we cherished both of them.

In those horse and buggy days, they took rooms during the winter in Washington but otherwise stayed in their old family home with Papa and Mama. They never married, and lived together until Aunt Annie's death of tuberculosis in 1905. The next year Aunt Mamie came to California to live with us, bringing a freight car of furniture.

One of my favorite stories told by my Papa Alonzo recounted a Civil War event that involved him as a twelve-year-old boy. While he shared the story directly with me, his mother had also saved an article printed in a Virginia newspaper that conveyed the event.

At the outbreak of the Civil War in 1861, Grammie, as well as Aunt Annie, who was about fifteen years of age, had taken a strong stand in favor of the Union cause. At first, their home was within the Confederate lines and communication with Washington was very difficult and hazardous. Forts constructed and arranged in a circle around Washington for the protection of the National Capital after a time drove back the Confederate lines a few miles. The line across the Potomac extended down to Arlington Heights and some distance below. Grammie's home, about a mile and a half from Fort Smith, fell within this line of forts and came under their protection. A number of Union regiments encamped nearby. They had great and growing needs, and little by little the family's timber, fences, stock, and crops disappeared until there was scarcely anything left save the house and bare land. The newspaper account declared that even the cook stove came up missing one morning.

Very frequently, Grammie awakened in the night to the sound of the "long roll." This long, continuous drum-roll signaled troops to fall in under arms, and served as a warning that action was imminent. When Grammie heard the drum roll, all of the family hastily dressed, secured what valuables they possessed, and waited in the cellar. Grammie and my two aunts were devoted to the Union, and they did what they could for the soldiers.

As my Papa told the story, he explained how one midsummer morning in 1864 he was playing with his dog on the porch. Grammie Hayes was resting in the sitting room and reading a newspaper. Aunt Annie was at her job at the Bureau of Engraving and Printing in Washington. Suddenly there came a loud, whistling sound, followed by a terrific explosion directly over the house. Grammie recognized the screaming noise as a shell fired from one of the heavy guns. Quickly another shell buried itself in the earth close to the house and burst, throwing up clouds of dust and dirt.

"I knew what that meant," Papa told me. He saw the New York Regiment (recently sent over to Fort Smith) putting up a target in our field. He figured out quickly that they had been firing at it. Another shell, from one of the huge siege guns which armed the fort, came ricocheting towards the house, striking the ground at short intervals. With a shriek, it plunged through the garden, destroying everything in its path. It filled the air with dust, gave two or three more skips and screeches, and then finally burst over near the road. Grammie instructed the children to go down into the cellar.

Papa said Eliza, the family Negro hired help, began praying to "de good Lord." Grammie urged my father, Alonzo, to run up to Mr. Pearson's just as fast as he could. "Ask him to go to the fort and have the firing stopped," she commanded. Considering the possibility of the house being struck and burned by the shells, Grammie thought it better that she remain with the other two children.

My Papa ran through what had been the garden, climbed the fence, and started to run with all his might towards Mr. Pearson's house, a half-mile distant. He had barely cleared the fence when another shell came tearing through the shrubbery and burst close to the house. One of the flying fragments struck him and knocked him to the ground.

My grandmother heard her boy cry out, and rushed to kneel beside him. Flesh from the back of his ankle had stripped upward, laying the anklebone bare. She hastily bound up the wound with strips torn from her clothing and set him behind a large chestnut tree, its generous trunk affording some protection. Two more shells struck nearby while she was binding up the wound. "I must go up to Mr. Pearson's before a shell strikes the house and burns Mary and Douglas," she cried.

When Mr. Pearson received word of the dangers to our family, he went in great haste to the fort. Grammie, along with Becky and Bertie Pearson aged seventeen and eighteen, ran back to check on her injured boy as shells continued to burst around them. Weak from pain and loss of blood, Papa was unable to walk. So Grammie and the two girls carried him in their arms as best they could. They waded the little stream in the hollow, and then carried him up the hill to the Pearson home, (stopping a moment to bathe his face and hands). By this time, Mr. Pearson had reached the fort and the firing ceased. Mary and Douglas came, and a few moments later, the regimental surgeon and hospital steward came galloping down the road on their horses. They expressed extreme sorrow at what had happened and treated my Papa's wound.

Papa always said he had begged his mama to sing to him while they sutured his wound and that he had sought her assurance that she would not let the surgeon cut off his leg. That evening an ambulance from the fort took my father home. The officers had done everything in their power to atone for the suffering they had so carelessly but unintentionally caused. The surgeon and his assistants attended him tenderly until the wound healed.

I often reread the faded newspaper article that called my father Alonzo a hero. It read in part:

> He was uncomplaining through it all; and the fortitude with which he bore his sufferings excited the admiration of everyone. The surgeon offered to procure a pension, but Mrs. Hayes declined, saying she was too thankful her boy was alive

to think of asking aid from the government. Alonzo was soon able to walk with the aid of crutches, but could not dispense with their use for many months.

Mrs. Hayes, now an aged woman, loves to tell of those perilous times. One of her daughters, a lady of rare qualities, fills one of the highest positions allowed to her sex in the government departments in Washington. She has in her little cabinet at home the very piece of shell which did its cruel work that day. It is rusty, and bloodstained. Alonzo limps a little, and will always have cause to remember the summer morning when the New York Regiment in Fort Smith bombarded his mother's house.

I was brought up on many tales of the Civil War, as related by Aunt Mamie (Mary Hale Hayes), then a teenager. She told of the Sunday when an Officer of the Day came to call. Grammie told him that her family always attended church, and she invited him to accompany them. Services held in a surviving building (a barn) meant a hot, dusty walk. The officer, a very short man, walked beside her with his sword fastened to his waist by a sash, and it clanked at every step. Aunt Mamie told how horribly embarrassed this had made her. On the way home, she felt shocked when the officer declared he had been married twice and desired her as his third wife!

Something amusing happened the same day that Aunt Mamie never forgot. Dress materials in those days of wartime were hard to find, but she had been happy over her new white dress with little blue flowers—blue had always been her favorite color. When she looked down at the new dress, she discovered the blue flowers were gone! The wartime dye had not been a success. At home, she felt a tinge of sadness as she hung the dress away in a closet. However, sometime later when she had reason to take the dress out again, she saw to her amazement the blue flowers were back! Apparently, the hot sun faded them out only temporarily, and the dark of the closet restored the colors!

An encampment of Union soldiers adjoined my grandmother's property, and as the war progressed, my grandmother felt much sympathy for the men there who were far from home. She showed much hospitality when sometimes soldiers on leave came to her house, knowing that they must get very tired of their monotonous food rations.

The ongoing war often brought drastic changes to communities. Sometimes Union soldiers tore down the floors from the schoolhouses to make floors for their tents. Mamie, only fifteen, went to live with an aunt in New England for several years in order to receive further education. We always wondered why Aunt Mamie never married. The tale among the family was that at one time her trousseau was ready when the engagement suddenly broke off. Another story was that when a certain suitor asked Mamie's mother for her daughter's hand in marriage, Grammie refused permission. "He isn't worthwhile," Grammie said. I surmised that Aunt Mamie went away not only for an education, but also for her safety from "unsuitable" admirers. My aunt told me of at least one occasion when her mother, seeing a soldier approach, sent her upstairs to hide.

At the time of the Civil War, both William Nairn Reed and his eldest son Boardman Reed wanted to enlist to fight for the Union, but they felt that one of them should stay home to care for the farm and their large family. The two men decided to draw lots, and it fell to Uncle Boardman to go to war. Wounded in the battle of Bull Run, my uncle was clearly proud of his G. A. R. (Grand Army of the Republic) button.

My parents' firstborn son, Alonzo Reed Hayes, only lived for four months. Hylinda, Alice, and I were healthy. However, our cherished brother Gilman suffered from a heart ailment, and our family determined that their only hope for his survival was to move to a warmer climate. I was nine, Hylinda was twelve, and Alice was only four when our family placed love for six-year-old Gilman above everything they loved about Virginia and our extended family. In December 1897, we headed out for California. Realizing how greatly I would miss not only the cousins who lived nearby, but also the two treasured aunts who remained in Virginia, I was heartbroken.

Uprooted from our precious relatives and the family history we had grown to cherish, we also left behind all of the places I had grown to love as a child. It seemed a desperate move to me. For five days and nights we traveled west on the train—my parents, my three siblings, and me. I kept a small journal telling of that trip:

December 15, 1897–

I got a letter from Aunt Annie. She gave us a prize box. The aunts packed one prize box for every day. I just now looked into one of them. Alice got a doll, Gilman got some alphabet blocks with pictures on them, and Hylinda and I together got a fun game. Hylinda got a kind of drawing book. Mama got a book of the Gospel of St. John. Papa got a jackknife and a comb.

Fourteen people came to say goodbye and to see us off this morning. This morning we passed through Alexandria where my Grandma Hayes was born.

A man and woman who have nine children are traveling also on this train. There is a China man and his little boy in this car. Papa says he heard that they had been all over the world, they are stage actors, and they can talk English.

Southern Pacific transfer across the Mississippi River- Photo courtesy of New Orleans Public Library

We are now in Orange Courthouse, a little town, the County seat of Orange County, Virginia.

We took big hampers of fried chicken and canned milk. Our train car had little berths for us to sleep in.

We are now on our way to California. I just now saw the mountains. I think they are the Blue Ridge Mountains.

Day 3

Last night we crossed the Mississippi River. It was a mile and a half wide where we crossed. I think the car had a track on the boat and they pushed the boat up against the land and the car ran up onto the car track on the boat. We came near to being left behind.

As the train traveled west, we began to experience the dry and barren landscape of the West. I was afraid our life would be just as barren as this prairie without our cherished aunts and cousins.

2

Discovering the Charms of Long Beach

Caroline
By Elsie Hayes -1904

When in the years to come we shall be old,
And our glad lives will be tales that are told,
May we remember schooldays of yore
The lessons, the old games, the mystical lore
Which mingle with fact in a little girl's heart.
The loves, and the longings—all these were a part
Of our happy school-life, far happier made
Because 'twas together we studied and played.

While our younger sister Alice was already learning to ride our horse, Gilman was not strong enough to do any of the things that other children thrived on doing. He needed to be pushed most places in his wheelchair and seemed to have no energy. I loved my brother, and the thought that he might get stronger made our move bearable. Leaving my cousins and my Aunt Mamie and Aunt Annie behind meant leaving a part of my heart in Virginia with them, but I reminded myself often that the climate in California might give Gilman the opportunity to do all of the fun things other little seven-year-old boys did.

I began writing some stories just for him, creating a hero named Gilman who was brave, strong and healthy. Mama frequently reminded me, though, not to challenge him to attempt to do too much. Her words helped me to remember that Virginia was now a part of our past.

We girls thrived in the warm California sunshine. We packed our winter coats away and happily replaced them with bath suits for the ocean. Living just a few blocks from the beach was a strange and wonderful new experience.

Long Beach, California, had incorporated as a city in 1888, the year of my birth. Nine years later, when my family moved there, it had a population of 1,500. Known for its long, wide beaches, Long Beach was advertised as a seaside resort community. Actually, it was a semi-arid landscape, and unlike Virginia, there were neither oak trees growing nor streams running past our home. However, the town boasted of twenty-four streets laid out in a neat grid and most of the necessary businesses to ensure growth. Long Beach had a city hall, bank, post office, high school, and elementary school, feed and livery stables, a hotel, public library and numerous churches. We soon discovered the Long Beach Bathhouse and Pavilion, the ice cream parlor, the Chautauqua Hall, a skating rink, and several restaurants. The Southern Pacific Railroad went right down the middle of Second Street. An exciting new experience for us children was watching the trains as they clattered through town.

We began our California years twelve blocks south of Signal Hill. Papa bought a ten-acre "farm" on a flat, treeless mesa near a bluff overlooking the Pacific Ocean. Little did we know back then that Signal

Hill would become one of the most productive oil fields in the world. My Papa purchased five acres for himself and five adjacent acres for his sister, Annie, who planned to retire from government service so she and Aunt Mamie could once again be a part of our family.

A number of large estates graced Signal Hill. It had a 360-degree view and was known for its cool ocean breeze. Fruits, vegetables, and flowers grew in the lower elevations. Temple and Eliot Streets bordered our farm, where Papa grew flowers and melons, and raised chickens.

Just twenty blocks west of Papa's fields, the municipal farmers' market sold fresh produce three days a week. Farmers, as did Papa, sold their wares and produce directly from their wagons. We were charged fifty cents for a six-foot space along the curb.

With all of that, Long Beach was not at all like Virginia or Washington, D.C. Oh, how we came to miss the wooded hills and valleys of Virginia. However, we sisters soon developed friends, and Gilman was included in many of our activities. In my box of keepsakes, a yellowed newspaper article reminds me of some of our early years in Long Beach. There is no title; the penciled date of 1900 meant I would have been twelve years old.

Wednesday of last week a number of small people were invited to spend the afternoon with the four Hayes young people, corner Temple Avenue and Elliot St., Alamitos, the occasion being a "dolls' party." Each little girl was armed with two or three dolls, each decked out in bewildering finery. A unique feature of the afternoon's program was the exchange of presents for the dollies, the manufacture of which had been carried out with Christmas like secrecy. The presents were displayed in an upper room which had been made ornate with paper boughs and flowers and consisted of hats, capes, necklaces, belts, laundry bags and a variety of other useful and ornamental articles, which, to judge by their pleased, though somewhat set smiles, were greatly appreciated by the recipients (the dolls). At four, dainty refreshments were served by Mrs. Hayes, assisted by Mrs. Howell.

Elsie with her doll Beth, Gilman, Alice and Hylinda

Even Gilman attended our dolls' party. The newspaper article not only listed names of the children who attended but also included the names of the dolls. Included in that list of attendees was my doll Beth.

At one time Beth belonged to a child who lived in a convent. The doll's wax head was close in size to that of an eighteen-month-old child, adding to her life-like appearance. Beth became mine, along with a large assortment of clothes, before we left Virginia. Originally, Beth had yellow hair, but as she was already eighteen-years-old when I obtained her, it was quite worn. Aunt Mamie's hair (shorn when she had typhoid) became a new doll wig. Beth was so lifelike that once as I held her on a streetcar, a woman remarked to her child, "Why can't you sit as still as that little child?" Beth's arms and hands were brown kid and the body was cotton.

I disliked the taste of the Long Beach water. Perhaps it was the smell of sulphur in the water that disgusted me. However, we discovered drinking the water from a toy teapot made the water less distasteful.

As we children grew older, we experienced many of the adventures Long Beach offered. There were frequent dances and concerts at the nearby Pine Avenue Pier. When I was in Long Beach High School, an Italian band used to play on the Long Beach Pike. The members of the band were young and handsome. My Papa knew that these young artists charmed many of the local girls. That disturbed him and he cautioned us, "Never marry a foreigner." Though we girls were brought up always to obey our parents, ironically we three would eventually all marry "foreigners." My older sister, Hylinda married an Assyrian man from Persia, Absalom Urshan; Alice married an Englishman (Ernest Burley, a wonderful brother-in-law to me), and I married Jack Roberts from Wales.

About the time I entered my final year of high school, the city built a magnificent glass-enclosed sunroom on the end of the pier. When it opened in February 1906, as many as 3,000 attended a dance in this parlor. Some months before our family moved to Long Beach, a whale washed ashore on the beach. The city cleaned the skeleton and placed it on display in the sun parlor. We were in awe of this sixty-five-foot skeleton of *Minnie the Whale*.

The Pike was a world-famous amusement area near the pier. The exciting Plunge, an enormous salt-water pool, provided entertainment beside the sea. What a sensation for us, as Eastern girls, to experience this pool, with its water temperature maintained at eighty-three degrees. I soon developed a love for swimming and for the beach. California had unique advantages unobtainable in Virginia. Three blocks down the street from our home, we discovered a cave hidden in the bluff above the beach. We girls would take a blanket and books and make clam broth while hidden away in our cave. In spite of our early misgivings, it was a delightful California childhood.

By 1904, the Pacific Electric rail cars ran three blocks south of our farm. The introduction of the rail cars became a huge success bringing visitors from Los Angeles to Long Beach. We often rode these electric cars to the Plunge, the Pike or the pier. The Pacific Electric Company also landscaped the bluff along the shoreline creating a lovely park area nearby.

Top left—Clark Cleaver with Elsie's family on Palomar; Bottom left—Hayes' Long Beach home; Right—Elsie wearing her Grandmother's dress, worn to the Inaugural Ball for America's 9th President William Harrison and then worn to his funeral one month later.

All three of us girls graduated from Long Beach High School, an impressive piece of architecture, opened the year before Hylinda attended. Life-long friendships developed during our high school years. Caroline Harnett and Ruth Stailey and I called ourselves *The Triumvirate* and we interwove our initials, just as our hearts had intertwined in friendship.

Among my treasured remembrances is Caroline's note to me:

Dear Elsie,

You must come out not only to Burnett [her neighborhood] but Harnett! We won't see enough of each other if you just come after school, so couldn't you come Saturday after dinner and stay until church time Sunday? I should just love to have you, and mother said I might because Josie is going to spend the night with a teacher friend of hers after going to see Shakespeare. If you couldn't come, of course come Friday or Thursday whichever day suits you best. But I do wish you could come.

I will look forward to it with so much pleasure. I wish I might have gone to the game and seen you, but I was really too awfully busy Ethel has a little go-cart for Gertrude and with her little creepers on she looks so cunning. I do hope you won't have to go anywhere Saturday I don't know what I will do if you do.

I must say good-bye now dear from your own true love,

> Caroline
> P.S. You simply must come!

I was devastated when Caroline died from a kitchen fire just weeks before I graduated from high school. The Long Beach Daily Telegram reported, *"The pall bearers were eight of Miss Harnett's schoolmates attired in white."*

I wrote poetry about my treasured lost friend. Friendship continued with Ruth (the other member of our triumvirate) until she died of tuberculosis while I was teaching school for three years in Arizona.

My beloved little brother Gilman became unable to walk—he simply did not have the energy. Pushing his wheelchair and reading him countless books brought us together as I watched his body grow weaker.

It seems to me tourism was so prevalent in the thinking of the Long Beach city planners they neglected matters of utmost importance to the community. There was a Methodist resort that occupied the entire block between third and fourth Avenues. On this property, the Methodist Church built an auditorium that could seat 1,700 people. It also served as a community-meeting center. It included a large bell that rang during emergencies, weddings, funerals, and school graduations. Yet in 1904, as Gilman was dying of heart disease, the city had not yet built a hospital, though they did have twenty physicians. Construction began on the hospital a year after thirteen-year old Gilman died on January 1, 1904.

After Gilman's death, we longed even more for the Aunts left behind in Virginia. Aunt Annie wrote to Papa:

January 30, 1904
1881 Third N.W.
Washington, DC

Dear Alonzo,

We were glad to get yours and May's nice letter written for Mary's birthday. I know we all have the same wish to be together in times of sorrow as well as joy and our desire may be gratified sometime. I hope Congress gives attention to superintendents and clerks and retire us as was recommended by the Civil Service Commission in its report this year. Although I am not superannuated or as old as the Civil War Veterans, my term of service has been longer and the length of service and age clauses will both be considered. I have no doubt it will be done sometime. When I am deemed too old to serve and legislated out, Mary and I will, I suspect, pull our tents and steal silently away to the Pacific Coast to end our days with you all. You may be in Berkeley, or you may have finished, and both your eldest daughters graduated and earning good salaries as teachers of higher branches or being authoresses or artists or singers.

We shall not be able to have as much to spend but can always sell an acre or so and live on that. This is what we aim to do and be comfortable and have those around us the same. We can probably have a cottage and live in comfort by you.

Our family has always been too prone to be satisfied with our own society—we enjoyed each other and it was a very pleasant way to do. But I guess it is right and better to have a few more of the right kind of friends, so as to have some congenial associates for you and May and the girls.

You are so much better off in your part of the state in having refined, cultivated people among your friends, people whose influence will be elevating and for the best in a spiritual and worldly way both.

Both Mr. and Mrs. Rathburn mentioned your advantages in that respect in your part of the state and intimate it is very different there with them.

I am sorry for them. That is what makes the Mid-West so unbearable, its wrongness in nature and in people—its newness. Your country might be as old a civilization as Virginia as far as its people and its appearances go.

We had 10 inches of snow yesterday morning and it fell in a day and night. It is now warmer and melting without sunshine. Yesterday it was down to 7° above zero, two above is our lowest we had last week and then it ran to 60° and melted almost, yet not entirely off and then this new one came. The cars however ran regularly, and we had no inconvenience and have been comfortable. We run two large oil stoves all the time we are in the house, which adds a good deal to our expense that we did not expect when we rented rooms. Nevertheless, the furnace is totally inadequate, the cars are convenient, and we must keep well and feel well to work hard all day so we don't complain.

I expect you like details of our doings as I do yours. Yesterday after breakfast, I took a car and a transfer to the Ninth Street South, rode to the south side of the market, and got out to buy a chicken from the countryman. I can't bear the thought of those horrid cold storage chickens, undressed. Alonzo knows how they looked stacked on the stands. I got just the nicest little one for $.50, looking as if we had dressed it at home the night before. Then I got on the car, went to the office, put the chicken out in the snow on a north portico until I was ready to go home, and stowed him in my pretty, red embroidered bag. After office hours, I went to get some money orders and bought some bananas and pink Tokay grapes. Sunday we enjoyed a good sermon on the first fifteen verses of Romans.

Love to all, Annie

3

My Palomar

From a Mountain Peak
By Elsie Roberts

Joy of the sun and fog, And of the moonlight clear;
Joy of the rain and snow, And wind that screams in fear;
Joy of that music sweet —In treetops heard, and streams;
Joy of the shadows deep, Where broken sunlight gleams;
Joy of azalea's breath, A heavenly ecstasy;
Joy of the world below, Spread to the shining sea:
Joys of the out-of-doors — Ah, they shall never fail!
God is a comrade here, On many a mountain trail.

My Papa was aware that the family longed for the lush, green countryside left behind in Virginia. Coupled with that was the terrible sadness over the loss of Gilman. So, in the summer of 1904 Papa decided that we would all benefit by a trip to the mountains.

"I keep hearing about Smith Mountain down in San Diego County," Papa said. "Hear it's a fine place to camp. With a good team we could drive there in three days and camp along the way."

Tales of Smith Mountain (later renamed Palomar Mountain) were irresistible. We chose a 120-mile horse-and-wagon journey along the Pacific coast and then inland across the coastal hills to the San Diego Mountains. Southern California maps for 1904 revealed long stretches with nothing but isolated ranches scattered between small communities.

That trip was the first of many our family would make. It wasn't always easy, of course. Bumping along in the summer sun, we had no defense against the heat. The dust of the stony, rutted roads turned to mud in winter rains. The load was always heavy with groceries, clothes, and bedding, besides five passengers. We passengers were apt to walk up hills and through sandy stretches. Near Temecula, there was a long, especially hard pull through heavy sand that we always dreaded. We were roughing it indeed, but there was adventure and charm in those leisurely jaunts. I shall never forget the meadowlarks singing from fence posts along the way. At night, our family slept underneath the wagon.

Before the trip, Papa gave us a warning. "It's going to be a hard pull for the horses. They'll be pulling their feed, our groceries and bedding, and us. Each of you may take only one apple box for clothes, books, and anything else."

Each of us carefully filled one box. The wagon was packed; the two horses harnessed; they were stomping and switching their tails. Papa, Hylinda and I climbed up to our seats, while Mama stood by the door with key in hand.

"Alice," she called. "Hurry! We're ready to go." Finally, Alice staggered out of the door, her arms so full of paper dolls, doll clothes, books and other extras that she could scarcely see over them.

"But your box is already full!" Papa protested.

"Oh, I'm going to hold these in my lap," Alice assured him, not realizing that weight was even more of a problem than space.

Soon after sunrise during that first trip up the mountain, I woke to feel my bed moving under me. "It's time for the horses' breakfast," Papa said. He smiled at my bewilderment. He was gently pulling out the hay spread on the ground under a quilt where we were lying. This became a regular happening on our trips from Long Beach to Smith Mountain.

Our drives would take us through countryside scattered with ranches and occasionally little villages. In the afternoon Papa would watch for a ranch where hospitality (or rental) extended to the use of water. He would buy hay for the horses. Hay was as vital as the modern motorist's stops for gas. We traveled in an open wagon drawn by a team of two horses. The country was so uninhabited in those days that you could camp most anywhere along the road. Nobody ever bothered you.

We would build a fire, unpack groceries for supper, and spread hay left for the team's breakfast as mattresses for our beds. Still trying to save weight, Papa would bring only enough feed for the night and the next morning by tying feedbags full of grain about the horses' noses. Papa grew to love camping so much we used to laugh about it and say he had gypsy blood.

Sometimes our last camp would be in a dry riverbed at the foot of the grade. The horses had been watered for the night at the nearby Pauma creek. In the morning, we needed only to dig a small hole in the dry sand beside the wagon, and water would rise in it. Then there was the six-hour climb up the old west grade, disrespectfully referred to as "Nigger Grade" for Uncle Nate.

In those days, the ascent up the long fifteen-mile west grade, going from 1000 feet in elevation to 5200 feet in fewer than ten miles, was by a two-horse wagon road. In some places, it became a fifteen percent rise—winding, narrow, and steep. Only at certain spots could wagons pass, so travelers soon learned to keep a careful watch for the possibility of another vehicle approaching from the opposite direction. The snake-like path of the road made that glimpse possible here and there. We climbed on endlessly, longing for release from the sun on those barren

Nate Harrison—Photo by Robert Asher

slopes. For weary miles it wound in and out and around, and always up over hills largely brown and dry except in spring.

We came to a curve where there was a spring and a watering trough under the trees, and a black man waving a friendly greeting. Nate Harrison, a freed slave who homesteaded a ranch on the wagon grade, served early travelers by providing water for the weary visitors and their horses. All of us enjoyed the memorable "Uncle Nate" and the refreshment from his spring in the shade of lovely oak trees. Uncle Nate would eventually become our friend and neighbor. The grade now bears his name.

Beyond Nate's cabin, we saw the forest. Oaks, evergreens, and giant ferns—it was heavenly and I fell in love with it at first sight. Though only sixteen years old, I knew it would be a love that would last me the rest of my life. Palomar Mountain became the object of my adoration. I often spoke of "the mountain" as some might say "my husband." There was no need for further clarification. The mountain looked so much like our beloved old home in Virginia we were all enchanted.

Alonzo Hayes & Mr. Moorehouse headed up Palomar

We had hungered for hills and trees, and our whole family fell in love with Palomar.

That two-week camping trip was a dramatic introduction to what became "our mountain." For the first trip, the summer of 1904, our family consisted of my parents, my sisters Hylinda age eighteen, Alice age eleven, and me, age sixteen. People walked for the most part, in order to ease the poor beasts' load. Walkers hunted for steep shortcuts from one zigzag to another.

On that first climb, we spotted a wagon on its way down, a speck twisting in and out on the curves above us. "Look!" Papa leaned down from the high wagon seat. In an urgent tone he called to us toiling hikers, "See if you can locate a place where we can pull out of the way!"

We ran ahead, panting. We looked in vain for a wider spot that we might soon reach. Then we saw the descending wagon was waiting for us — so far ahead that it was some time before we reached it. There the roadway was just enough wider so that we could pass. Our horses had shied. They weren't accustomed to steep passes and we assumed that the sheer precipice had startled them. Then we walkers stopped in astonishment. No wonder the horses had shied. A tree was tied to the back of the wagon, dragging in the dust.

The passing driver grinned at our amazement. "Hi, folks!" he said. "I guess you're greenhorns. That tree is an extra brake, holding back where it's so mighty steep. You'll use one coming down." Farther on we nodded knowingly when we saw a wilting, bedraggled evergreen cast aside at the foot of a particularly sharp drop.

After resting, we began our trek again—now through beautiful forests where unknown shrubs, ferns, and wild flowers entranced us. That first time we came to Silvercrest (now State Park Headquarters) we seemed to know instinctively we had arrived. I remember vividly that the mountain belonged to me from the first moment we reached the top and our wagon stopped on the crest. Running through the woods to the edge and seeing the world spread below in unutterable beauty, I can never forget my exaltation. From that first moment, Palomar was mine, and I was at home.

In those years before smog, the mountain also received more rainfall, close to sixty inches a year. Beyond the open slopes covered with ferns and dotted with wild flowers, the evergreen forest swept down and

Smith and Douglass Hotel—Photo by Robert Asher

42

away. Farther on, back of the lower hills and the valleys with their few villages, white surf edged the vivid blue of the Pacific. Catalina and the Coronado Islands stood out sharply on the horizon. We were almost delirious. Only a wing of the twenty-mile long mountain was called Palomar at that time. The Smith and Douglass Hotel was located at Silvercrest, with a campground across from the meadow near a spring. We set up camp there and loved everything about this place— the crisp mountain air, the clear, cold water, and the infinite, profoundly satisfying beauty.

Sometimes we hiked and sometimes we drove to the post office at Baileys. We came upon Iron Springs where stones and tree-roots were bright orange, and then past a fast flowing stream. We explored Doane Valley where Old Man Doane lived in his log cabin. We visited Lower Doane where campers vacationed under the giant pines near the rushing Pauma Creek.

After such a climb, campers usually chose to stay awhile at the beautiful campgrounds at Baileys and Iron Springs. Not only did Baileys have the post office, it also had a summer resort and a small grocery store. The Bailey store sold things like horse collars, straw hats, overalls, blue denim shirts, and gloves. They also sold provisions like beans, flour, potatoes, sugar, honey, lard, baking soda, bacon, cheese, and crackers.

We set up a dinner-plate-sized campfire for noon coffee in the great, grassy, tree-lined Mendenhall Valley. We had heard that the Mendenhall Cattle Ranch covered 9,000 acres and they had 1,200 Pole Angus cattle. But we had no idea that we were trespassing on private property until Mrs. Mendenhall, the ranch owner, accosted us.

"Destroying the cattle feed!" she said. She didn't know how conscientious Papa was about fires and that he always made great effort to assure they would not spread.

We drove on toward the Frazier sisters' ranch. Suddenly the horses snorted and Papa pulled on the reins. A huge mountain lion was drinking at a spring only a few yards ahead. He lifted his head and looked at us.

"I'm not much of a hunter," Papa said in awe. "There's only one shot in my gun. If I fire it, I might only wound him."

We stared breathless. Would the lion attack us? He stared back, then turned majestically and walked away.

One night another wild creature caused excitement at our camp. Everyone was awakened by the sounds of another camper screaming. The mountain air was particularly chilly that night, and a rattlesnake had

Aunt Mamie –Mary Hale Hayes

crawled into her warm bed. She sprang up unharmed, but we were all more cautious afterwards.

Papa soon purchased the 160-acre Mack place. It was chiefly forest with seven acres of apple orchard that he later increased to fourteen acres. He paid $5,000 for the ranch that included a house, a large barn, and the apple trees. For the next nine years Papa would spend the summer and fall of each year tending the apple ranch. From that time on, the mountain became our second home, and we spent joyous summers there. After my first introduction to Palomar until my senior year at Pomona College, I thrived on summers high above the valleys.

Every September, we girls were driven down the mountain for school and college. After 1906, when Papa's sister Aunt Mamie came out from Virginia to live with us, either she or Mama went back with Papa to keep house for him during the apple season. The other stayed in Long Beach or Claremont with us girls. In the spring, Papa and

Mama or Aunt Mamie went back to the mountain for the planting. In June when school was out, he drove down to take the rest of us back. After the apples were picked in the fall, we closed the house for winter.

Alice spent the fall on the mountain just after she finished eighth grade. She attended the little country "school in the woods" near Iron Springs, where the Bailey and Mendenhall children also attended. During my teen years, the community held dances in this schoolhouse. The Mendenhall boys wore cowboy boots and their spurs dug holes in the floor. Sometimes those from the east end of the mountain danced until daylight so they could see their way home over the bad roads.

One time, the Mendenhall boys came galloping past on their way back from a cattle drive, trying to hide behind the trees. Their shirts were off and back then, even men were modest!

As a girl, I loved to ride horseback. Mother never made us ride side-saddle, but we had to wear heavy divided riding skirts—each division was a skirt in itself. When we dismounted, we buttoned a flap across so that it seemed we were indeed wearing a skirt. Of course, it reached all the way to the ground and made walking very difficult!

Some horses were unpredictable. One time on our way to the mountain, the new horse in our team kept balking. We were all concerned. Suppose he refused to go up the Grade, or balked on that steep and narrow road edged with precipices? In a trade at a wayside ranch, Papa was able to acquire Mack, scrawny, old, and one-eyed, but ready to go. He had once been a racehorse, and when I rode him later, he proved it in a glorious but terrifying way.

A balky horse wasn't the only thing that could delay us. There was the time, as we neared the mountain, when the wagon tongue broke. Fortunately, we were near the tree-bordered San Luis Rey River, so Papa made a pole out of a strong sapling, and we were able to proceed. A blacksmith's shop, forerunner of today's garage, was available in some places. There the clang of its anvil added to such pleasant sounds of travel as the creak of wheels and leather and the thud of horses' hooves.

Sometimes on our trip up the mountain, we followed the coast as far as Oceanside, but usually we went inland. There was no mad rush

then, and countless things gave us pleasure. The horses ambled or trot-
ted, and we saw all the ground squirrels looking at us from fence posts
and the singing meadowlarks that swept overhead. In those days of
greater rainfall—and less civilization—wild flowers were unbelievable.
In springtime, there were fields of yellow violets, baby blue eyes, tidy
tips and poppies; and the mustard grew high.

We liked to make our first night's camp by the lovely Santa Ana
River. The clear shallow water overhung by trees was fairly warm in
summer. We had the place to ourselves, and we girls would put on
some of the old clothes for mountain wear and bathe in delight. Always
fascinated by the Greek myths, I pretended that I was a water nymph,
frolicking in that wild spot.

During our first trip, Papa stopped the horses as we met an
oncoming car in the Temescal Canyon. Those strange unknown
"machines" were apt to startle horses into running away. Polite drivers of machines stopped and waited until horses were safely past. This
driver waited.

"That's our Mr. Hatch!" Mama exclaimed as we came closer.
Despite his cap and goggles, we recognized our Long Beach banker.
We weren't really surprised that this should be Mr. Ellsworth Hatch, a
fellow member of the Long Beach Presbyterian Church, the first man
in Long Beach to own a machine. Such vehicles were so rare that even
this far from home, it was not surprising that the one car we encoun-
tered might be his. Our surprise was more about this amazing contraption having traveled so far!

Incidentally, I well remember how thrilled I was when one noon-
time that same kind gentleman, driving past Long Beach High School,
stopped and offered a ride to some of us youngsters. Though we only
went a few blocks, it was terrifying as well as exciting. We traveled all
of fifteen miles an hour.

The Temescal Canyon was always hot in summer, but in early
summer, the Matilija poppies there were in their glory. Their tall, proud
stems held huge white blossoms. In the month of June, Papa would
come down from the mountain to take the rest of his family back up

for vacation right after school closing. He would stop at Temescal and gather sheaves of those plentiful and most beautiful flowers. There was no law against picking wild flowers then, and with more rainfall during that era, they were more plentiful. Papa had been a florist in Virginia, and he knew how to care for the poppies so that they arrived in Long Beach fresh and lovely.

It used to be the custom at Long Beach High School for friends of graduates to bring flowers to the ceremonies, practically all of them from home gardens. Junior girls would receive them at the door and heap masses of them at the edge of the stage. No other graduates received such spectacular bouquets as special friends of the Hayes girls to whom we gave those magnificent poppies.

When I graduated from Long Beach High in 1907, perhaps because I happened to be valedictorian, I received so many flowers that we all carried armloads out from the Long Beach Auditorium to the surrey. For overnight, they were placed in a big portable washtub and various other large containers. Gone indeed are those provincial but delightful days.

The trip up Palomar was hot! I recall vividly feeling "baked" after hours in the uncovered wagon. The tiny town of Corona was hot, too, and Elsinore was hotter yet. There, on that first trip, we were overjoyed when we stopped to call on friends. They offered cool drinks from a big clay jar called an olla. It hung on a shaded porch covered with wet burlap.

Because of its mineral water, the little village of Elsinore, built along a wide lake, was a health resort from the time the Indians used it for that purpose. Many health seekers came for the baths, but the water when warm made a horrible-tasting drink.

From Elsinore, we journeyed slowly on to Temecula, pitying the horses because of the long stretch of sand through which they had to struggle. The Pala grade between Temecula and Pala was a rough, narrow road down the wild, rocky canyon. Indians passing that way used to pause near a certain spot where enormous boulders still seem to topple, one behind the other. There they would call to the spirit of the canyon asking permission to continue on their way. If an answer came, they went on; but if they heard no answer, they turned back. We used to rest the horses there and call out. If we stood in an exact spot, sometimes echoes answered us.

The Indians were not the only ones who sometimes felt a sense of insecurity in their travels. When gentle little Aunt Mamie came to live with us at the age of sixty, camping was very new to her. The first night out on our way to Palomar, she looked thoughtful as the beds were being spread. Then she suggested mildly, "I've always slept with a roof over my head. If I could empty a grocery box . . . ." A bit like the proverbial ostrich, she soon lay down for the night with her head in a wooden grocery box. "Now I'm all right!" she said contentedly.

In Aunt Mamie's New Testament, she made brief notations about those trips.

Started for Palomar—Smith Mountain—June 27, 1907. Westminster, Anaheim, Olive. Camped in a barley field, edge of Santa Ana Canyon for the night.

On the next page she wrote:

Friday, June 28—Through Santa Ana Canyon, Yorba, Rincon (Mexican settlement), Corona, Temescal Canyon all night, by a ditch which takes water from mountain springs.

The notes go on:

Saturday, June 29- Elsinore, by a lake 3 or 4 miles long. Wildomar, Murrieta, near hot springs. Temecula, Pala Canyon, down Pala grade, Pala mission, through canyon by San Luis Rey River. Camped in Mr. Weaver's stockyard, wire fence kept out dogs and a multitude of black pigs. June 30- Sunday Pauma, Pauma Creek. Camped on Pauma reservation and rested on the Sabbath day Monday, July 1-Up the 15 mile grade to Palomar!

At the end of the summer of 1907, we moved from Long Beach to Claremont where my parents had purchased a house. Except for the time spent at Palomar, we lived there for two years—Hylinda's last two years and my first two years at Pomona College. Meanwhile, Alice went through the eighth grade and spent a year at Pomona Preparatory School. We were nearer the mountain now, and the complete trip to the ranch could usually be made in three days.

On one occasion, Aunt Mamie wrote, "I went on cars [train] with children, left Palomar Sept. 10, 1908, and reached Claremont Sept. 11." Her entry means we were driven to Temecula and from there took the Santa Fe train.

That year, after the usual autumn trip to the mountain, Aunt Mamie and Papa went back later during a chilly season. She wrote, "Alonzo and I left Claremont Dec. 5, camped in shed at school house at Temescal. Next night camped near Temecula by roadside, frost on our pillows and comforters when we woke in morning. Third night camped under splendid live oak tree at Nate's. Alonzo made big campfire. Arrived safely at Palomar Dec. 8, 1908. Returned to Claremont Dec. 24, arriving safely." There was a time Aunt Mamie wrote of reaching the ranch at 8:30 p.m., once at 9 p.m., and one April, "Reached Palomar Saturday morning 1 a.m.! Safe and sound." My parents made one trip up the grade leaving the foot of the mountain at 4:30 a.m. and were home at 2 p.m. with mother walking almost to Nate's cabin.

One day in the summer of 1906 there was a general mountain picnic at Rainbow Falls (since then destroyed by floods). We were returning through the woods when suddenly we heard a most startling sound. Incredulous, we ran to where we could see a bit of the upper grade of Palomar. There indeed was a machine grinding its way up, the first car we had ever seen on Palomar! Eventually there were automobile races on the steep west grade. They were all run by timing the entrant from the foot of the grade up to the mountaintop. One car would race up the mountain one day; another would go up the road the next day. Whoever made it in the shortest time was declared the winner.

When we first came up to the Mack place, we were not acquainted with anybody in the area. "I've heard that there is a mountain feud," said Papa. "Don't take sides."

We saw much more of the Baileys than of the Mendenhalls, but became close friends with both families. The eldest Bailey daughter, Nanny, was married and gone, and I think Hodgie Bailey was already in San Diego working for Jessop's. It seems to me that Orlando Bailey was also away much of the time. I particularly admired him when I was a teenager, and he was much older! Clinton Bailey was the big one and then Milton Bailey must have rivaled him. I remember once looking at Milton (I think in a hammock) on our porch, and marveling at his size. All these were older than I. Milton, born in 1884, was four years older. Of course, since I was only sixteen when I first met him and he was a mature twenty, he seemed much older.

The youngest Bailey, Elizabeth, was my age to the year, the month, and the very day. That intrigued me.

Theodore Bailey was postmaster until his son, Milton, succeeded him. We were all much impressed with the way the father of the family, Mr. Theodore Bailey (even after we thought of him as old) would still literally run between his house and the post office, which was in the yard. The post office was one room with a window in the door, through which mail was passed.

Later, after Baileys built the dance hall, they had dances twice a week. The Bailey family always hired a cook who would make all her own pies, and baked her own bread. There were berries of all kinds, lots of fruit, and lots of milk and cream. For breakfast, they served fried eggs and bacon served family style. They served a full meal for lunch and then a big dinner at night. They hired someone to take care of the

Bailey Home and Resort.

garden and raise the vegetables. The resort opened on Memorial Day and closed after Labor Day.

The original Bailey Homestead was constructed of adobe from their backyard. The Indians at the foot of the mountain came up and built the house. Mr. Bailey had not only orchards but a wonderful garden, growing with great success such things as we had known in Virginia, but not before in California: currants, different varieties of raspberries and gooseberries. My mouth waters to remember them. I think it was from Mr. Bailey that Papa got the start of our rhubarb, a superb kind, pink, juicy, and flavorful.

We girls would take turns going over for the mail three times a week. We'd go horseback or afoot, often with cross cuts, or by the road along the edge of the mountain or with the one from our place to Sunday School Flats. That road was the regular route continuing to Doane Valley or the schoolhouse or to Baileys.

The Baileys were a religious family. They held a Sunday school at the schoolhouse on Palomar for a while and Mr. Bailey was superintendent. If Mr. Bailey was absent when we were up there, Papa substituted for him. Papa had been a Presbyterian elder for many years. I remember teaching a Sunday school class of small children outside under the

Elsie on Horseback at ruins San Juan Capistrano Mission

trees. People would travel by wagons, or afoot. Everyone was amazed when once a San Diego couple from the Bailey resort appeared in an elegant buggy with beautifully fringed top. Once we went to a vespers service out on the Baileys' wooded hillside.

It was there at Sunday school that I first met Miss Alice Parker, afterward a most dear friend of mine. She introduced herself to us because she heard that I was to enter Pomona College that fall where she was an instructor. It must have been around 1910, after we were close friends, that she came up to the mountain with Ed Fletcher, a family friend. He went on to the Bailey resort where she had stayed before, and she spent the night with me so that we could have a good visit.

Our side journey to the Guajome Ranch was probably a part of one of our travels by way of Oceanside, our alternate route between Long Beach and the mountain. In 1906, we camped not far from San Juan Capistrano Mission, no doubt the first night out from Long Beach. It was near the beach in a wild, isolated spot and that night coyotes howled nearby. My dear friend Caroline Harnett was once going with us to spend a month at Palomar. Accustomed to her huge family, she had never been away from all of them for overnight, nor had she ever slept in the open. I remember her terror at that weird wailing, which I still love to hear anywhere. Once in passing near the Capistrano Mission, we spent some time at its ruins. A Kodak picture shows me on horseback among the fallen walls.

Sometimes there were mountain picnics for everybody up on the mountain, or evening campfires for residents and campers and hotel guests (if a resort was open.) Everyone sat around blazing logs. Dear old Mr. Cleaver and George Doane had their special performances. Mr. Cleaver enacted a story about a flipped pancake that landed on his head and left him hunting it. Mr. Doane did a musical number in which he illustrated the differences between an ordinary song and what he called a *"hanthem"* that repeated words and phrases over and over.

I think it was that first summer at our first community campfire that my parents had been warned to guard their daughters from the well-known mountain bachelor, George Doane. He was older—much older—but that did not stop "old man Doane" from seeking a young bride. My parents listened as the mountain gossip spread that he might make a play for one of us Hayes girls. My parents carefully sat us three girls on a log by the campfire with Papa at one end and Mama at the other end, allowing no room for Doane.

The following summer Doane traveled to Louisiana and brought back a sixteen-year-old bride. Along with the young bride came her Negro servant, Amy. I chuckle each time I tell the story of first meeting Amy. Our Hayes family had Negro servants in Virginia but since coming to California, servants had not been a part of our life. For me perhaps the entire arrangement of fifty-something Doane marrying a sixteen-year-old girl was not as much a novelty as was Amy. She was tall and had large feet. Once after Amy had walked past barefoot, I removed my shoe and stood with my foot inside Amy's much larger footprint. Mama was embarrassed that I drew attention to Amy's large feet and immediately reprimanded me. Later Amy was given the nickname "cubby" due to the size of her feet.

The young bride's mother was a widow and perhaps a better match in age for him, though even she was younger than old man Doane. This new mother-in-law was also named "Hayes." When Doane had first applied for a mail-order bride he had numerous replies from women

Clark Cleaver in his orchard; George Doane in his cabin—Photos by Robert Asher

who were interested in a man boasting of owning much fine mountain property. In fact, when Doane went to Louisiana he had his choice of either the widowed mother or her sixteen-year-old daughter. He chose the daughter and eventually Susan Hayes, her mother, decided to come to Palomar Mountain on her own. She homesteaded 160 acres and tried for some years to make a success on the mountain.

My mother was somewhat embarrassed because the widow, bearing the Hayes name, had applied to be the future Mrs. Doane. George Doane had a long white beard of which he was rather proud. That young girl used shoe dye to blacken the famous beard. Eventually she divorced him and her mother gave up the homestead. History records Doane's character was perhaps darker than his beard.

My parents allowed a sense of freedom and adventure that prepared me in the years ahead to live life fully and without fear. There were indeed dangers on the mountain (besides an occasional character like George Doane) like steep terrain, mountain lions, and rattlesnakes to mention a few. Yet, our parents allowed us to walk alone to collect the mail or ride horseback through the woods. They were secure in their faith and did not waste their energy on life's unknowns, and life on the mountain was definitely full of unknowns.

Alice was five years younger than I, and she stayed on the mountain with Mama and Papa the year that I finished high school. As a thirteen-year-old, she had romance on her mind and was keeping a close eye on the schoolteacher and Milton Bailey.

Palomar Mountain California May 18, 1906

Dear Elsie,

I got your nice long letter a few days ago. Thank you for the pictures. Last mail day I got a card from Long Beach post office asking for a cent more postage, and so I haven't gotten them yet.

Last Tuesday I got eight pictures of animals from Hylinda. One of them is that one "three members of a temperance Union," three horses drinking at a trough. It is very pretty. I made a panel of them here in the front room. She also sent me her embroidery hoop to use and some embroidery silk.

School is lots of fun! I have gotten four books out of the library: Emma Lou, Mrs. Weeks of the Cabbage Patch, Lovely Mary and Stories of Colonial Children. I like them very much. They have fine books. I think maybe I'll get The Mill on the Floss.

I think our teacher, Miss Penn, is lovely, and so does Milton Bailey, apparently. They go horseback riding. I have seen them or heard of it two or three times and every time Mr. Bailey was away! He, Milton, escorts her to school sometimes. I saw them once and once she spoke of his setting the clock that morning. I have tried to beat them there, but haven't yet. Yesterday noon when I got back from the post office there he was on horseback beside the porch talking to her (he had apparently brought her a letter) but he rode off before I got quite there. He was at the post office when I left it, so I guess he did not stay there at the schoolhouse very long.

Now I had better get down to business. Did you get my coral cross mended? I wish you would get my bank emptied sometime when you are downtown. Please tell cousin Nan to get light blue hair ribbons for me if she writes to that woman who she got her ribbons from. I hate to ask you to do so much business for me, but don't hurry if it is not convenient for you. I want to get some slippers for my doll. On the way up here part of the way she was in the bundle in the top of the wagon penned up, and once she fell out and the only harm done to her was that the sole of one of her slippers came off! Wasn't that wonderful! It got mislaid or something. I think Momma did not take it out of my pocket and washed my dress or it was lost out. Anyway, one of Muriel's slippers is missing a sole, and it looks kind of ragged and bad. I wish you would get me a pair. I think I would rather have black ones or maybe white, you can use your own judgment. Please don't pay more than a quarter or not much more or I'm afraid my dough will give out. You see, I haven't paid Papa for my roller skates yet because I didn't have my money out of my bank. You can pay for things out of that money, and if it gives out change bring it up to me. Papa said he would pay me $.50 if I found a bee tree, and he could get on a swarm.

It is good Mr. Sibley is back. How does he look and preach now? When is he going to the Gen. Assembly?

Please excuse scribbling.
Lovingly, Alice

55

4

Mountain Heights Untouched by Fleeting Times

Greetings from Palomar
By Elsie Roberts

If you might climb our mountain peak, in all this wintry weather,
If we might roam the snowy woods and follow trails together,

Then—but you are too far away, this happy Christmas season,
So I send you a mountain gift, with friendship for the reason.

I cannot send the bare brown oaks gray squirrels have just forsaken,
But here are empty acorn cups, from which the feast was taken.

I cannot send the mountain breeze through all the hemlocks singing,
I cannot send the hemlock trees, nor birds above them winging.

But here I send a little spray from giant hemlock broken,
Of faithful love, the evergreen has ever been the token.

I cannot send the great gray rocks heaped up in silent places,
Where lovely ferns amidst them grow, like sudden smiling faces.

Yet last night at the edge of dusk to find this gift I wanted,
I slipped away to Faerie Wood, by the wee wild folk haunted.

I gathered ferns among the rocks (One last oak leaf was falling),
I gathered hemlock cones and sprays. (Was that a lone bird calling?)

Up from the depths the gray fog stole, through the still branches trailing.
The world below had vanished quite, and twilight too was failing.

Peace and beauty, enduring strength, untouched by time's swift fleeting—
These are thoughts from the mountain heights,
Sent as my Christmas greeting.

I adored riding, and often it fell to my happy lot to make a good part of the trip up Palomar in that way. A saddle horse lightened the load for the team, and it seems to me that I rode more of the way than my sisters. Nowadays, when in half an hour by car we race across the old Santa Marguerita Ranch between the Capistrano area and Oceanside, it reminds me how long that thirty miles used to be. I recall how hour after hour all day long our horses toiled to cover it. I see myself on my saddle horse riding alongside or a bit ahead across that endless lonely mesa. One such time we saw no one all day long except a cowboy or two in the distance and a Mexican driving a buggy on our same narrow, dusty road.

I remember an adventure while riding with Milton Bailey and several others. I was on Mack, an old one-eyed former racehorse. It was fun riding him because he went so fast. This time, though, he went too fast. When Milton started to pass me, Mack, trained never to let any other horse be in the lead, suddenly shot ahead at top speed. Though I loved to ride, I was not an expert in the saddle, and my feet flew out of the stirrups. I feared the horse might throw me any second, so I lunged across his back, twisting my hands in his mane—anything to be able to hang on. Of course, he slowed when far enough ahead to satisfy himself. The boys were amused!

One day a blazing fire erupted on the lower part of the mountain. I took the news to Silvercrest, riding bareback on our burro. Papa had gone with the team to help fight the fire to save my mountain. I prayed, dug in my heels, and galloped to tell the people.

After our first trip, Papa continued to travel back and forth to the mountain. Mama's scrapbook reminds me of what those trips were like. She included in her memory keeper an article written by Papa for the newspaper entitled:

"Camp on Palomar Mountain" April 3, 1905

Alonzo G. Hayes, of 2801 Elliot St. writes from Palomar Mountain, Nellie Post Office, San Diego County, "Mrs. Baird, Mrs. Hayes and I, after we left Long Beach, stopped overnight

at Perris and the next morning we met Harold Oliver at Temecula with the team. He left Long Beach the day before we
did, having driven through the Santa Ana Canyon. We left the
auto at Temecula and all proceeded by wagon, camping the
first night on Pauma Creek, 5 miles east of Pala. Next morning
we started up the grade, the upper part covered with clouds.
On driving into them, we found first fog and then light rain.
We arrived at our ranch before that night. The fourth day after
this we found 4 inches of snow covering the ground. Three
days later the depth of the beautiful snow had increased to 30
inches. We had to melt snow to obtain water for our horses
and ourselves. On April 17, we enjoyed a fine sleigh ride. The
elevation here is between 5,000 and 6,000 feet, making it one
of the finest apple districts in the state."

I had served as literary editor for the school annual, and I enjoy
looking back through its pages. It was hard not to be proud of Long
Beach High women's basketball team who were champions for the
league in 1907. The yearbook shows five girls dressed in matching
middy blouses with below-the-knee skirts. Dark stockings covered
their legs and each had her hair adorned with an oversized bow. The
young men had a baseball team, and both gentlemen and young ladies
enjoyed tennis. The debate team consisted of four young men and one
young lady. Eighteen students participated in the mandolin and guitar
club with eleven playing in the orchestra.

On June 21, 1907, I graduated from Long Beach High. Chosen as
valedictorian, I gave my speech as if addressing the figure of a smolder-
ing fire. The newspaper described that metaphorical speech as "brief
but eloquent." The graduating class consisted of eighteen girls and sixteen young men.

Even after completing high school and going on to attend Pomona
College in Claremont, I still made the trek up Palomar as often as
I could. One night journey up the old grade in December 1909 is
unforgettable. In fact, that whole trip is etched in my memory. We
were again living in Long Beach, but for the first and only time my

Top—Maypole 1907, Long Beach High School; Left—Hylinda in the garden; Right—Alonzo with girls in car.

parents were trying out the idea of spending the winter at the ranch. We girls would join them for the holidays. Hylinda must have been at Los Angeles Normal School that year and for some reason she did not go up to Palomar for Christmas. Alice was staying with our friends, the Hands, and attending high school in Pasadena. I was a Pomona College junior, living in Sumner Hall, then the girls' dormitory.

A few days before Christmas, Alice took the Santa Fe train at Pasadena. I got on the same train when it stopped in Claremont, and Papa met us with team and wagon in Temecula. My poor Papa was

1907—Elsie graduation Long Beach High

evidently coming down with a heavy cold and reached Temecula bent over with lumbago. He was ten years older than Mother, looking older yet because of the beard he always wore. That evening when we registered in the funny little hotel in the otherwise almost wholly Indian settlement of Temecula, he looked ancient.

Alice and I shared a room down the hall from Papa's room. Mama and Aunt Mamie were alone on the mountain, and a storm was coming up. We had to drive on up the next day, and Papa asked me to rub his bad back with liniment. The eagle-eyed landlady stopped me when she saw me going through the lamp-lit hall to his room.

"He *is* your father?" she asked grimly.

Astounded, insulted, and highly amused, I tried to reassure her and showed the liniment. Dubiously she allowed me to continue.

Cold as it was, Alice and I were such fresh air fiends that we opened a window in our little hotel room. We struggled in vain with the one through which we saw faint moonlight coming through the clouds.

Another window, which showed no light, resisted our efforts at first, but eventually we managed to shove it open a little way. Relieved that at last we had some air, we still were restless, wishing that in this Indian village we were nearer Papa's room.

We awoke in the night, alarmed, and looked out to see an Indian standing under the moonlit window. We finally fell asleep but awoke in the daylight to discover that our opened window led only into a stuffy little storeroom!

Breakfast was early as we had a thirty-mile drive ahead of us. However, we were only on the lower reaches of the grade when dusk fell. It was bitter weather. We all wore heavy coats but the icy wind chilled us through and through. As usual, we girls walked part of the way up in order to save the horses. When we climbed back to the seat, we were glad to pull the heavy quilts about us that Mama had thoughtfully provided.

"It's going to storm all right." Papa looked at the black sky surrounding us and spoke in a hoarse voice. "It's getting so dark I can't see the road," he continued. "One of you will have to walk ahead and carry the lantern."

We put the thick quilts over our heads and fastened them under our chins with big safety pins. Our loving mother must have sent down those pins, too. As we walked along the edge of the road, the howling wind caused our shawls to billow out like balloons and almost blew us over the precipices at the lower side of the grade. We took turns carrying the flickering lantern.

The horses bent their heads and toiled ahead. Papa, bearded and muffled, bent, too. On that dark night, there on the bleak mountainside, I thought we must look like the Russian peasants I had seen in photos. Almost sixty years later that scene is still vivid to me.

We reached the forest and finally the ranch with its warm fires and warmer welcome. For days afterward, Papa was very ill. Later, Mama said it must have been pneumonia, and for a time we were greatly worried.

The snow fell silently for days. Mama and I went out with an ax and cut down a Christmas tree. Aunt Mamie filled our stockings, as she always did for Christmas, with contents earlier ordered from Sears and Roebuck—the Farmers' Bible —Alice brought it out for reference on every possible occasion.

Papa was better by Christmas Day. The sun was brilliant across the deep snow, and I walked over to Baileys for the mail with a firm crust holding me up.

Right—Alice and Elsie circa 1909; Bottom—Hayes barn with tall fir trees

For many years, mail came to the Nellie Post Office at Baileys three times a week. The carrier and his horse trudged up the old trail, an almost impossible trek. The mail carrier, holding on to the horse's tail, was pulled up the steep incline. Regardless of holidays or weather, whenever humanly possible the carrier with his loaded saddle horse came up the incredibly difficult trail. That year Christmas was a mail day.

I could never forget the beauty of that Christmas day. The storm was over. Never again, I fear, will there be such beauty on our mountain as on that pre-smog day when we had actual rainy seasons. Beyond the verdant hills and valleys, the ocean glittered with the distant islands standing out sharply in deep blue.

On that sacred day in the midst of such beauty, my heart sang as I walked lightly on top of the snow through that shining world. Christmas gift packages and greetings that I carried back only added to my always-remembered joy.

However, when it was poor Alice's turn as mail carrier two days later, the sun had done its work and the snow was starting to melt, and

Mail Carrier, Mr. Jolly—Photo by Robert Asher

she sank through deep clogging snow at every step. Though we used to take a shortcut over the hill, it was too much. She came staggering back, arms full of delayed parcels, and without a word dropped onto the couch and burst into tears. We were frightened until we realized that nothing had happened to her except exhaustion.

My parents decided a Palomar winter was not for them. When we girls were due back at school, the roads were still impassable. Our good neighbors, the Baileys, devised a possible way to get down once Papa was well enough to travel. The horses could manage the snow with less difficulty with their load lightened, and now the three eldest members of the family added to the load. So Alice and I went by Baileys' sleigh as far down as Lone Fir. From there I rode on to Temecula with another storm-delayed traveler, a young man from Alaska, who enchanted me with tales of the Alaska he knew. I felt charmed by the young man himself and at the same time tried desperately not to be tossed off the very high seat of his huge wagon. It had almost no handholds to help me when we hit deep ruts and stones washed down by the storm. We girls were a week late for school and college.

That was probably the time we stayed overnight in a quaint hotel in Capistrano—a Spanish style with balconies hanging over the road. "We'll leave early in the morning," Papa said. "We won't wait for breakfast. We can get that at El Toro." I rode the saddle horse, but it was so cold my feet felt frozen, and I got off and walked to warm them. El Toro was then only a tiny grocery store with meager wares. The only thing we found to buy for breakfast was soda crackers, so we munched them and went on.

In those days, any Pomona College student reaching the campus late after a vacation had to apply formally for readmission. My dear friend Alice Parker was still on the faculty there, and she told me with much amusement how when my application was read at a faculty meeting there was great astonishment. Never before in that sunny Southern California institution had the faculty seen the excuse of being snowbound for a week's delay in returning after holidays. However, she knew Palomar herself, and was able to convince her associates it could well be a valid reason. Whimsically, she added to me that my character might have had something to do with their acceptance of the excuse.

Our travels up and down the mountain were a great opportunity to experience the culture of Native Americans. There was a night when I felt alarmed by the appearance of Indians in Temecula as we camped near the town. We girls slept in a line with Papa at one end and Mama at the other. I believe Papa had a gun at his side for added safety. In addition, sometime in the night we became aware of several Indians standing near and looking at us. Those days were not so far from the time that Indians signified danger in people's minds. Of course, many Indians showed friendship and kindness.

There was a time at a Pala fiesta when our family stopped to see a ramshackle little old merry-go-round set up for the occasion. We girls just had to take a turn, while reluctant Papa watched like a hawk. The Indians seemed so honored to have us share their fun that they refused to let us pay the merry-go-round fee.

A fiesta in Pala was one of the highlights of one of our trips. I will never forget seeing an Indian rain dance to the moon god. Several very old women stood in a row, apparently oblivious to onlookers. Two had faces most deeply lined with wrinkles and were said to be at least 100 years old. They were barefoot and wore Mother Hubbard dresses to their ankles. They lifted their eyes to the sky as they chanted and sang. These women took the lead in the weird chanting while the others shuffled and swayed, one after another, without apparent signal or change in the music. It took us to back to earlier times.

Coming home from Palomar in September one year, we reached the stream near San Onofre after dark and hastily made camp. Next morning my mother looked at my blotched face in shock. Did I have smallpox or scarlet fever? We soon realized that the mosquitoes had chosen me as their special target. I was still a mess when school started a few days later.

Many of my mountain memories seem linked to the various families we first met there. One evening when we were calling on the Baileys, Clinton Bailey did something that made their dog howl in a way that sounded just like singing along with his master, a practiced trick that was very funny. Clinton seemed to have what we called a crush on a cousin of ours who visited us one summer. Alice, in recent years, informed us of an accident she had never made known before. She and the cousin went haying with Milton and another boy. When the girls were on top of the hay wagon, in fun this boy thrust his pitchfork into the hay closest to Alice. It was too close, for it went deep into her thigh. She made no outcry and did not mention it at home, afraid our easy-going but extremely protective father would be too angry with the boy. Until it healed, she would slip off at intervals and pour peroxide into the deep wound. There was not so much talk of infection back then.

Then there was the mountain dance that Louis Salmons gave at Silvercrest when he was a widower, and a housekeeper was caring for his five little girls in that big old hotel. I think the event was in honor of his daughter Louise's first birthday. Earlier Papa had agreed hesitantly that at least once he would take us to a dance at the schoolhouse. He and mother would chaperone us, and we were positively not to stay late. I rather think it was our very first summer as mountain residents, and our parents were not quite sure what a mountain dance would be like. It was indeed very different from anything we had ever attended before. Young men slipped outside now and then. We came to understand later they went to get "refreshment" from a barrel containing "spirits!"

I have no recollection of the Baileys at that dance, but perhaps it was because they would have seemed more like everyday people—what we were used to. I do know that certain people startled us with their behavior and that first encounter remained in our memories for years.

Maybe the Baileys did not attend. I do not know when they started having a resort, but I will never forget a small share in that busy and very popular place. It was near the end of the summer, probably in 1908 or 1909 when Milton came over to our ranch one day with an urgent request. I remember practically his exact words: "I put myself at your mercy. The two girls who had been working for us have to go down because normal school is opening. Does Pomona College start later? Would two of you girls come over to help us, just for a week? We do not want to close the resort 'til then."

Alice's high school had a longer vacation, too. She and I went with a sense of great adventure. We were very naïve. Certainly, I never dreamed that someday my husband and I would have a little Palomar resort, too. Now we girls anticipated the experience of guests treating us as servants. It would be fun to play the part, as if we were actresses. We did not know then that it was common for college girls to work at mountain resorts. Anyway, it would help Milton, and we would be earning money—five dollars apiece for the week!

We were almost disappointed when the only person who treated us as menial servants was a little dressmaker from the village of Escondido. She had probably scrimped and saved for a long time to have this week or two as a hotel guest. We had a lot of fun out of that.

The other guests were wonderful to us. They were a fine group of people. One owned an outstanding San Diego store; one taught at San Diego Normal School. They seemed to love the Baileys as well as the mountain, and there was a happy atmosphere. We had never been half so busy, rushing from early morning until night, with a little time off in the afternoons. We set tables and waited on them, washed dishes, and acted as chambermaids in the tents that were the guests' bedrooms. These were scattered among the trees on the hillside and required us to bring pails of water to fill the pitchers and the bowls.

We surely enjoyed the week. Miss Hodgie, Milton's sister, was his helper that particular summer, and she was a darling and a delight. She was a lasting influence with her warm friendliness, her wonderful mixture of swift efficiency and bubbling gaiety. She made the kitchen work a joyous task for us. In sunny mountain mornings, when the guests came into the dining room for breakfast, their cheerful "good morning" added to the feeling that the day would be right.

No doubt this unexpected week increased forever my awareness of gladness, typified always by our dear little Aunt Mamie's favorite quotation, "How far that little candle throws its beams. So shines a good deed…." In old age, I am profoundly grateful for this. And as always, the mountain itself meant, as it still means, an inexpressible happiness.

Milton was young to be such a good manager. He was very thoughtful of Alice and me. On at least one evening, he came to the kitchen door: "You girls hurry with the dishwashing," he said. "We're holding the dance 'til you're through."

As a part of his resort services, Milton ran a stage drawn by four or six horses until the time came at last for motorized vehicles on the mountain. In the early days, he or his driver used to tell the passengers, as they approached within distant sight of Uncle Nate's place, that they must look up and watch for something. "See something white way up there? That's Uncle Nate's teeth shining." To be sure, the dear old Negro used to sit out on a rock to see anything coming up the grade, and of course, it was actually a white rock seen from below.

There were two old roads to Doane Valley, one running from the west grade, and the other running from our ranch through the woods towards Baileys. It came out above Sunday School Flats and turned across the flats. That unused road is still there, as is the one turning from the flats to Baileys.

Early one morning the girl who was visiting us and I climbed into a back seat of Milton's stage. No other passengers were on board at the time. He took the way through Sunday School Flats, whipping up the horses as he neared the little gully with its sudden deep drop and sharp turn beyond. I knew the worst part of the ride was coming up, so I turned to the other girl. "Hold your breath!" "Never mind about your breath," the young driver said. He grinned as he dared to glance at us over his shoulder. "Hold your seats!"

Like her husband, Mrs. Bailey must have been extremely capable, raising well all that family in such an isolated spot. I do not recall much about her except when she was alone, I went over to stay overnight to keep her company. I still remember vividly the charming little room under the eaves where I slept in their old adobe house beside the little post office. Later, I think they raised the roof and added another story. Crisp white curtains hung at the windows. All the way around the top of the walls, just before the ceiling slanted down to them, there was a row of autumn-tinted wild strawberry leaves, deep pink and red. They had been gathered with care to get the loveliest (I know from hunting such in the fall), then beautifully pressed, mounted, and I imagine shellacked. I still recall them with delight. It was Miss Hodgie's work.

The Baileys not only had the post office but also a little store. Hylinda made graham bread to be sold there one summer.

Milton must have been on the mountain more than his brothers and sisters. At least he was more in evidence. One night he heard that honeymooners were camping in lower Doane Valley, and he organized a chivaree. Some of us went in Milton's stage (so it must have been after the Baileys' resort was started) and we were well accompanied by outriders. Beyond Sunday School Flats, the road ran along the edge of the woods beside the valley. It was a beautiful moonlit night, and the woods darkened the narrow stony road. It was a charming spot, and we were in high spirits. When we finally neared the honeymooners' camp under the great pines and near Pauma Creek, we quietly crept up on them. Suddenly we let loose with a wild racket close beside the lone tent. We rang sleigh bells and pounded on tin cans. Someone beat an anvil and others fired guns. It was an appalling noise in what had been a silent night. The couple ran out alarmed.

I am still sorry for the poor young couple, who seemed utterly unable to cope. Shy country youngsters from somewhere below, they were overwhelmed. Then, somebody started a chant: "We won't go home; we won't go home 'til you give us something to eat!" It was more or less the custom in those barbarous days—food followed the racket. The chant went on until in desperation the young bridegroom said awkwardly, "We're going down tomorrow and we don't have anything left to eat. Would you maybe like a drink of water anybody?" We were so mean that we filed in a long line past their water bucket, each taking a swallow from the tin dipper. At least a large portion of us continued the line repeatedly, around and around, in the lantern light. Somehow, back then, it seemed romantic and a great lark.

Many interesting people claimed Palomar as their home. When we first came to the mountain in 1904, we met Robert Asher, a thirty-six year old bachelor, who had arrived the year before. Over the next two decades, we came to know him quite well. He was an artist, a fur trapper, and mineralogist, and he kept a detailed journal describing the other residents on Palomar. I laugh now when I read his recollections of our family:

The coming of a Hayes family made quite a change in the social life of West-end Palomar. A. G. Hayes and his wife were very charming people to say nothing of the vivacious and no less charming daughters three, also Aunt Mamie. Aunt Mamie was a charming little body, always cheerful and, more to the point, one of the best—if not the very best—of my customers in those early days when I was making them and trying to sell various photo views of mountain folk and scenery. One summer Mr. Hayes was greatly disturbed over the inroads of the veritable plague of gophers. He tried various means in an endeavor to get rid of them, but the gophers had proved too much for him until Aunt Mamie came to his rescue with an offer to trap them herself. "Good." said Hayes, "I'll give you ten cents apiece for all you can catch." Mamie answered, "Hurrah, I'll take you up on that!" Aunt Mamie received credit jotted down that one summer for over 300 gopher pelts.

I tinted some 5 x 7 photos and she paid me the advanced price without winking an eyelid. I made up some nifty little cedar-bark frames and mounted some of the black and white views in them. Aunt Mamie took to them instantly. All in all, I am afraid a very large portion of $.10 pieces pulled out of gopher holes went into photo card and photo print gifts to friends living in less favored sections than Palomar Mountain. The Hayes family was hospitable people and I was often a dinner guest, an overnight guest (a time or two) when Mr. Hayes was alone on the ranch, once in a heavy snowstorm. This was the time I caught a photo of A. G. with a pair of snowshoes slung over his back.

One hot and very sultry day I was going to the post office when I met Ed Bish, the forest service ranger. It had been thundering for some time toward Morgan Hill. I had just noticed a suspicious looking bit of smoke and I at once called his attention to it. He had not seen it before but after a

Robert Asher Tinted Print in Cedar Bark Frame

moment's study, he declared that there was a wild fire behind it and down the mountain south of the Smith and Douglass hotel. I glanced at the smoke again and then affirmed that I did not think the fire was south of Smith and Douglass at all, but was south of Morgan Hill down my own canyon. Ed was stubborn and insisted it was down south of the hotel. Finally, he got a bit huffy and began giving orders. He said he would ride up to Boucher Hill to get the lay of the land, but I was to go direct to Hayes ranch and call out Hayes on fire duty and report with shovels and axes at Smith and Douglass.

Hayes was home when I got there, but he objected quite strenuously to any forest ranger ordering him around. However, he finally subsided and we sallied forth armed with axes and shovels bound for Smith and Douglass straight up over the hill. In the meantime, a thundercloud had formed overhead and we were not yet halfway to our rendezvous when the whole sky just about dropped itself about our devoted shoulders. We cut for the shelter of the nearest tree trunk, but it was no good.

Robert Asher——Photo by Robert Asher

"I'm wet through." shortly declared my partner in distress. "I'm going home Bish or no Bish," and off he started. "Better come along and dry off," he added "I have some extra underclothes you can put on." And so we scuttled back to the ranch Bish or no Bish. I never heard a word of complaint out of Bish, but I reckon he got a good soaking too— that is if he did not get down to the Bougher house in time.

And was there a fire and where? Certainly, there was a fire at the foot of the mountain right down my canyon and directly south of Gomez flat. The lightning had struck ahead of the storm and the fire had raced up the mountainside almost to the flat when the oncoming rain hit and flattened it out right there.

Hylinda attended Pomona College for two years before I graduated from high school. So it seemed natural that I too would also attend this prestigious school. Our family moved to a home in Claremont, near the college, and that brought them closer to Palomar Mountain. Papa still spent his spring and fall working on the apple orchard there.

The Virginia reel (a folk dance) was the only dance allowed that brought both sexes together at Pomona College. Girls had fun dancing together in the recreation hall. There was an annual Dove Ball, for girls only, when we wore our most attractive ankle-length dresses. On one such occasion, we wore masks. Suddenly we discovered among the party slippers a pair of men's shoes and a strikingly tall girl. Horrors and delight! I do not remember the penalty for that—or for the certain awful breaking of the rules.

Sumner Hall was then a girls' dorm. There was a strict rule that by 10 o'clock on weeknights all residents must be horizontally between the sheets with the lights out. However, once, possibly more often, one girl came back from an evening's entertainment later than 10 o'clock. The place was locked and dark—so she tapped on the ground floor window of a friend who cautiously opened the window and helped the miscreant enter.

Everything about college life thrilled me. The literary society voted me in as an officer. There were frequent plays and frolics. The societies included a men's organization, a women's organization, a literary society, debating club (including the Southern California Inter-Collegiate Prohibition Oratorical Society), Lyceum, Alpha Kappa, Kappa Delta, Sigma Beta Eta, YMCA, YWCA, the Student Volunteer Movement (Overseas-Missionary Society), Astronomical Society, Biology Seminar, Der Deutscher Verein-German Society, Prohibition League, and Society of Pure and Applied Mathematics. We had choral groups, dramatic groups, and athletic groups. The college had a band as well as orchestra. Activities filled my years at Pomona. The college was known for its customs and traditions—"Our Tribute to Christian Civilization," the college motto.

The men played football with seven other colleges. Track, baseball, tennis, and basketball rounded out the sports. The women played tennis in almost floor length white dresses. The men wore long pants as tennis attire. The year I graduated the college added a women's basketball team.

The college buildings were impressive. The outdoor Greek theater, built while I was a student, presented four dramatic productions each year and could seat 3,000. There were forty-two graduates in 1913

Pomona College Library

when I completed my years at Pomona. Actually, I was a part of the class of 1911, but our family doctor had advised taking two years off proclaiming I had *fragile* health. Possibly Mama and Papa were overly cautious due to losing Gilman in 1904.

Our family left Palomar in 1910 and it was some eight years before any of us again lived permanently on our beloved mountain. Papa travelled back and forth from Claremont and Long Beach. He eventually sold the ranch to the Hewletts and Esther Hewlett turned it into a butterfly farm. The post office moved there, too, with Esther as postmaster.

Our cousin, George Homer Reed, came to Long Beach for an extended visit before Gilman died. He was six years older than I and almost the same age as Hylinda. He enjoyed his visit and we did, too. In 1906, he married Belva Wagner. I saved the amusing letter that he wrote to remind me of our early years in Long Beach.

Wendell, Idaho December 23, 1913
Dear Aunt May and Uncle Alonzo and Hylinda and Elsie and Alice,
    We received your Christmas card and were glad you remembered me. I am sorry to confess that I am very slack in the matter of writing, but really, I think of you all very often. You treated me so well when I was

with you that I do not believe I shall ever forget it. However, I did want to shoot those long legged birds that flew up and down your seacoast, and the whole Hayes family objected to it.

I did shoot some though finally, Hylinda was sick one day and didn't seem to know what she wanted to eat, so I sneaked over to the beach and shot some of those bacon-type birds for her, and you thinking I did it out of kindness of heart, let me go unrebuked. Well, I confessed now, and anyway, I think the birds were intended for food.

Moreover, I remember Elsie in her plain and fancy swimming stunts. In addition, Alice specialized in croquet and on the pony that you had. In addition, I remember the dog that the little boy, Gilman, had loved. I remember thousands of other things about you, too, and all of them good, so you see I have not forgotten you, although you may have concluded years ago that I had.

When we get through selling apples, we are all planning to come see you again. Frank Howdles family included. We live just a mile from the Howdles and we certainly enjoy having them so near. They are very nice and we visit back and forth a great deal. They will eat Christmas dinner with us again this year. Each of the three years that we have been here, we have been at their home Thanksgiving and they have been here Christmas.

Frank is driving a school wagon this year, we take our daughter Helen up there each day, and she goes to school with him. Marjorie looks after her, so we do not worry the least bit about her. Harmon also attends school, but he tends to the telephone central evenings, so we do not see much of him. Belva wishes to be remembered to you.

We are going to have roast pork for Christmas dinner. We shuffled him off yesterday, Belva says not to tell you that she cut her finger helping scrape him. Now we do not want you to think that we are compelled to have pork for Christmas, for we are not. We have some geese, but we raised them on a bottle, Belva says, or some such tender tie as that, and she will not stand for their demise. Incidentally, there are no turkeys in the country and jackrabbits are too common to be delectable.

We have all enjoyed remarkably good health here. Scarlet fever broke out in the school recently, but the school closed immediately until the danger was past. Mother has been sick a good deal this fall, but she is much better now. Leta Kinney Garner remained with her while she was sick. I think Leta is still there but we have not heard lately.

Please remember us to Chas and Anna, and Gertrude and Uncle Tom and to Uncle Boardman and family.

With best wishes for a happy new year.

With love, George Homer Reed

I wanted to go to Berkeley to complete teaching credentials after I graduated from Pomona College. Finances required me to work to earn the funds to accomplish that goal. At age twenty-five, I applied at a Los Angeles employment agency and became a "mail order teacher," traveling in September 1913 to Cornville, Arizona, where I taught for a year in a one-room school on the banks of Oak Creek.

Arizona changed me. I was indeed a bit of a snob before going there. I loved literature and culture. Arizona transformed me; teaching barefoot, burro-riding children in Arizona became a challenge and a delight.

In one letter home, I referred to some of them as being "common and needing baths." As I learned to love Arizona's wild countryside and the children, my attitude dramatically altered. Developing an admiration for the character of these back-woods farmers, ranchers, and their children, I learned to view them with respect.

My mother would read my letters and then pass them on to Papa, my sisters, and Aunt Mamie. Later, mother returned all of the letters from Arizona to me. I saved them, bound with a faded blue ribbon, tied and untied numerous times through the years. As I read back through these letters and my diary, it reminds me how free-spirited, young, and in love I was at that time. I fell in love with Arizona, turned down one marriage proposal, and accepted another. Those three years in my mid-twenties were unforgettable.

In my letters, I described the Arizona years as "glorious." Yet I experienced isolation, lack of modern conveniences, and sacrifices. There remains great joy in the memory of those years. During those years, I

Published by E. Beck, Jerome, Ariz.   Marks-Fram Co., Los Angeles, Cal.

Jerome, AZ, circa 1913

learned to refuse to dwell on the hard circumstances. I chose instead to focus on the joy found in the adventure of a challenge.

After my year in Cornville, I accepted a high school teaching position in Williams, Arizona, for two years. Williams, a booming railroad town, had the social life that Cornville did not. Twenty-eight years old, knowing I wanted to return to California and begin a family of my own, I said "Yes" when a charming young Welshman asked me to marry him.

5

Clouds of War—
Times of Change
1917-1918

Woman's Heart
By Elsie Roberts

My heart was like a homing bird
That longs in vain for rest,
And cannot find it till it finds
Its mate, and builds its nest.

My heart knew many lovely things,
Yet always passed them by—
Went on and on through endless space,
Like wings against the sky

But now! Content—oh, jubilant!
The bird sings at its nest—
And oh, my heart has found its mate!
His child lies on my breast.

My Welshman, Jack Planwydd Roberts and I were married on a Monday, Christmas day, 1916, at my family home in Lake Elsinore on the ranch Papa had recently purchased. War clouds generated a dramatic foreboding of change for our world. We knew our marriage would certainly bring changes, most of them eagerly anticipated. We were both almost twenty-nine years old.

Our first year of marriage began on an uncertain note as far as Jack's job. In addition, we were not certain where we should live, and if he would have to go to war. I tried to maintain a sense of normalcy while dreaming of a future beyond the ominous threat of war.

My journal chronicles our new life together:

ENTRIES FROM MY JOURNAL 1916

On our wedding day, the living room was lovely, decorated with green and white. Mr. Hunt performed the ceremony with only the family there. Alice's Ernest came, and then we celebrated with a Christmas wedding dinner and the tree. First honeymoon night at Armsbury Hotel, Elsinore.

The day after Christmas, we left on the early train through a snowstorm for Los Angeles. We found an apartment to live in, and felt settled here. We are very, very happy. We began reading the Bible together. On Wednesday, we delighted in a restful day. We rose late, had only two meals, went to the hippodrome theater, and then early to bed. Our married life so far is gloriously happy.

Jack had to start back to work on December 28. I got breakfast before six and went back to bed when he had gone. It became fun getting dinner and having him come home to it.

Day after day, we have an early breakfast, and I go back to bed for needed extra rest. Today after the weather cleared, I had a walk, bought an alarm clock and groceries. We are so happy.

We received an announcement of marriage of my former roommate Mildred and Mr. L. Their marriage took place on our wedding day. I went downtown. I am sorry for my friends who are not married!

New Year's Eve we went to Long Beach where mother is visiting Alice. We celebrated with dinner there at Alice's home. Alice's little Dorothy is cuter than ever, and the baby Ernest Jr. is fine. Jack and I had a restful evening. Read aloud.

ENTRIES FROM MY JOURNAL 1917

JANUARY

New Year's Day—Los Angeles—Happiness is being together, today is a holiday for Jack. He rested and read. I enjoyed cooking. We went for a long walk together in the afternoon. Reading <u>Great Expectations</u>. I am so happy to know that my former roommate, Minna, also married on December 25th.

Shopped at Ralph's Grocery again, and began running a bill at the Denver Grocery. I am learning ever so much about housekeeping. I am the proverbial bride. It was a year ago I met my husband! It is wonderful to have Jack come home every night, and to find him there every morning! Housekeeping, accounts, etc. are great fun. I enjoyed making pineapple fritters. I naturally keep making new things, and Jack always eats them manfully. Delighted to have so many letters and gifts to acknowledge. I especially appreciated Mrs. Hurst's letter from Arizona, remembering how she once hoped I might marry her son Karl.

How differently Minna and I would talk now of our "affairs of the heart!" We are richly blessed. I do want to make a happy home for Jack. I rejoice in his evening comfort, reading, etc., and then we have wonderful hours together. We surely have a time making both ends meet, but I really find that interesting. We are together—that is what matters. We heard again from Jack's family in Wales. These cold mornings Jack turns on the gas soon after five for heat, and then comes back to bed. I get up about 5:30 to get breakfast. Then after he is gone, I go back to bed and sleep another two hours or so.

FEBRUARY

February 5th—Alice's birthday. Hylinda came to lunch, and I thought she was going to bring a poor woman she found in trouble. I enjoyed Hylinda very much. I began again reading <u>The Breath of Life</u>. Household work, then I did errands in town. And always my dear Jack in the evening.

Jack brought word that they transferred him to the San Pedro yard, at Terminal Island. We are glad. I had to do some more packing. Our last day in the little apartment, our first home for our first six weeks of marriage.

We moved to a barren mud flat called Terminal Island (formerly Rattlesnake Island), as that is where the Los Angeles Terminal Railway ended. The island became home to a thriving fishing industry with many Japanese-American fishermen. Terminal Island is our home for now.

Jack had been involved in the lumber industry since leaving Wales in 1904 at age 16. While living in Canada and Minnesota, he had worked as a lumber cruiser, examining timber stands to determine their potential value. We met and fell in love while Jack was working at a lumber mill in Williams, Arizona.

On February 12, we settled in at 109 Riverside Place, Terminal Island. After a rushing time we came from Los Angeles on the morning train and began to be settled in the three-room cottage—luxury after a one room apartment. Jack went to work at San Pedro lumber mill on Terminal Island at noon, and I went to San Pedro for errands. Sea air feels good after the city air. Settling in, and San Pedro again, I enjoy the ferry ride.

I walked to town by the boardwalk route and by the sand dunes in the morning. Walked on the beach in afternoon, and lay among the dunes to rest. Especially enjoyed Jack in the evening.

Shrove Tuesday. Made pancakes for breakfast in honor of Jack's Welsh memories of that tradition. I am learning other things besides cooking, too.

MARCH

Thankful for another payday. I made Jack's favorite Mulligan stew.

Jack still sometimes tells tales that are most entertaining for our evening's pleasure. I am reading <u>Martin Chuzzlewit</u> with great interest. I do not understand what the matter with my health is. I did not feel very well, and tried to take things easy, so I did not make many preparations for mother, my first guest.

On March 7th, I went to Long Beach, met Ernest, Alice & the babies, then mother and celebrated Dorothy's birthday at a beach picnic. Mother came back to Terminal with me.

Two days later, I found myself in the midst of awful pain, and then I knew that if all had gone well we should have had a baby, now lost. Had wondered before but thought from my contrary symptoms that could not be my condition. It hurts us both, but we think it must be best. Most providential mother was here. The next day was a strange long day on my back. Mother, bless her heart, will stay and nurse me and keep house for Jack. I try not to grieve too much, etc. Jack is very lovely to me, and our love for each other is wonderful. This hurts him, too, and naturally, we think of hopes for the future.

After a week of bedrest, I sat up in bed a little. Read in my diary and thought over my life. I pray again for forgiveness for all that has been selfish and wrong and thank God for great blessings. He has made me, through Jack, more normal. I want to be better too. As I rest there is plenty of time to think now. I do not deserve to be so happy, but I will try to be more worthy and more unselfish.

When he came home, Jack carried me into the living room and I wrote some letters. Jack began tinting the cottage. Stayed in the living room, but had my meals at the table with the others, appreciate feeling better. Jack read to me from Exodus and talked to me for hours. Lovely.

After only six weeks on the new job, they laid Jack off for the day as the rumors of war have made the lumber business fairly come to a standstill. He worked in the cottage, hard. We are so happy!

Now, after only one day at home Jack is back at work again. I really began to study Welsh, and Jack helped me turn an old notebook into a textbook with alphabet, vocabulary, etc.

A week later Jack laid off again half the day, so he worked on the cottage. Papa and mother left by the Ford in early afternoon to go to Alice's home, now living with her growing family in our childhood home in Long Beach. They stayed overnight on the way home to their ranch in Elsinore. Hated to see them go. Then I worked hard so I wouldn't be too lonely. They are so very good to us! Good to have Jack coming home. I dread the thought of war. Read from Tennyson aloud. Our bookshelves made by Jack now look inviting, almost filled.

APRIL

On April 3rd, we read President's Woodrow Wilson's speech in the paper declaring war.

For Good Friday, I swept the flat, made hot cross buns that Jack liked and planted flower seeds he got for me.

World War I is fully declared. I hope and pray all the war may end soon. I did shopping for Easter dinner at San Pedro. I saw a big gun being moved, making the war news all that more real.

On Sunday, we took the early train to Long Beach joining not only Alice and family as well as Hylinda, but also Papa and mother, who came day before from the Elsinore ranch. We all went by machine to Alhambra for Uncle Board's 75th birthday party. Twenty-nine relatives and connections came for the celebration, lovely time.

MAY

 Mr. Dan Hughes, queer and most interesting old Welshman, had dinner, the afternoon and then supper with us. He is a prospector, mineralogist, and a fascinating talker, with dignity, courtesy, and language chiefly of culture, but he looks exactly like a hobo.

I worked in the garden while Jack began remaking an old couch. Then Jack and I went to San Pedro to hear Chautauqua lecture on "What America Means to Me" by Arthur Walwyn Evans, a distant cousin of Jack's. It was a splendid lecture and real Welsh oratory. We were sorry he could not stay over and visit us. All my work is a pleasure because of Jack and the happiness. I received recipes from the Welsh mother.

Towards the end of May, it rained again. We transplanted some radishes. My morning: one and three-quarter hours of housework, one and three-quarter hours garden, one and one-half hours letters to home, one half hour to the village. While fishing, Jack caught a delicious crab.

I wrote once more to Wales. Made scones by mother-in-law's Welsh recipe. I began <u>Oliver Twist</u> again. Tried making Honey Tarts. We fought ants.

I read Dickens again. Though the war is in our thoughts, surrounding us with so many uncertainties, life continues to bring us joy. Jack works, we read, and I cook and garden. The simple life!

JUNE

Jack registered for conscription on June 5th with all other non-enlisted men aged 21-30. I went to 318 Temple Avenue, Long Beach, where Alice and her family have recently moved. Hylinda and I were nurse girls, etc., helping Alice to settle in since she keeps busy with two-year-old Dorothy and eight-month-old Ernest Jr.

Elated to be at Sumner Hall, Pomona College, Claremont. Here for class and alumni meetings and went to military drill with Alice. Splendid baccalaureate. The spirit here calls us to courage and sacrifice for the principles involved in the war, and I feel more ready for it. Talked of Oak Creek with Mary Beck who also taught at my former school in Cornville. Rejoiced in communion service. A long walk and talk with Alice was glorious.

While in Pomona, we called on many friends. We left early and came home where, despite what it meant to have been at Claremont and Pomona College and to have seen Alice, it was good to be with Jack, best of all by far.

Aunt Mamie & I went to San Pedro to get things ready for our cottage into which two Japanese have moved. The wife is refined and very dainty. We talk of going to Palomar. I wrote home with our thoughts about Palomar. We cleaned house. I made cake & puff paste. Jack, Aunt Mamie, and I all three sat on the beach in the beautiful moonlight.

JULY

I am making blue armbands for Jack. The bands identify those men waiting for the notification that they must join up.

Draft Day—July 20, Jack evidently not yet called, though many familiar names are in the lists.

We learned positively today that Jack is not in the first call, and I am grateful. Yet, I feel sympathy for our neighbors. I read that they have drafted three million men and one million men volunteered. Vigilante groups are rounding up slackers and 14,000,000 men have registered with the Selective Service.

On Sunday, I went to Sunday school. Five Swedes called. I led Christian Endeavor, with the subject "Golden Rule" and then stayed for church. Wish we could all be at Palomar together. Such plans as we are making these uncertain days! We talk late of Palomar plans.

AUGUST

I hope Jack will not decide to go to the mines in Montana. The copper mines are in full wartime production. Just a few weeks ago, 168 miners died in Butte, Montana.

Jack went to L.A. to see about position at Army camp in lumber work.

On Sunday, I went to L.A. with Jack. Went to Welsh church while Jack went to see about the position in New Mexico, and he decided against it. Came home and did Christian Endeavor.

Went to Long Beach to take mother a phone message from Papa. He has decided not to trade the Elsinore place, so we hope to go there soon. Jack left Hammond's Lumber Yard this a.m. and went to look for other work.

 Jack tried to sell our cottage place here and looked at new jobs—easy for him to find, though he cannot find one that suits him here, and I fear I am settled. The thought of moving for a fourth time in eight months is daunting.

Jack began night work at shipbuilding plant August 24, with twelve-hour shifts.

I heard that Alice & babies plan to go this weekend and join Ernest in Phoenix. Alice gave me baby things. How strange I feel! It is very hard to say good-bye to her and the babies, especially Dorothy. How changed the children will be before we see them again. So much is uncertain these days.

SEPTEMBER

Sept. 1—I came to Long Beach to discuss Jack's suggestion of moving here for our remaining time before we move to the ranch in Elsinore. We decided to follow that plan. I went to Sunday school and said farewells to my class.

Mother and I packed and then came here to 318 Temple Avenue, Long Beach. We lived in this house as children and Alice's family have now just been here. Papa and Mother went to L.A. to hear evangelist Billy Sunday, and were disappointed that he was too hoarse to speak.

OCTOBER

On Oct. 5, Jack stopped work at Los Angeles shipbuilding yard. Five days later, we moved to my parents' ranch at Elsinore to assist the war effort as farmers.

Concern has arisen over who would go forward with food production since much of the farm labor force left to join the war overseas. Now the government has deemed agriculture to be a part of the war effort. As America has mobilized for war, the government asked for voluntary compliance on the part of farmers, industry, and consumers. I gladly joined other young women recruited for the farm labor effort. Herbert Hoover has charge of this important program. I take my role seriously, "Hooverizing" like the patriotic slogan suggested, making "war" bread, doing "meatless Mondays" and "wheatless Wednesdays," volunteering with the Red Cross, and knitting garments for the Belgian war babies.

Jack is digging a new well. I am setting the rabbit traps and herding the five goats. Using dynamite, Jack and Papa got down about 17 feet in the well.

What joy putting baby things into my hope chest! I began reading Canfield's Bent Twig, an interesting picture of family life. Aunt Mamie & Hylinda drove Joe to church.

At the end of the month mother went with me to see Dr. Shank. It made my wonderful expectation of a baby more real. I liked the doctor. Went to a Red Cross afternoon where we "snipped." Jack did good work on the pipeline and cleaning the cow pen.

NOVEMBER

November 8th Water in the well, now at about 40 feet. Sunday, Papa and Mother went with Mr. Hunt to Laymen's Missionary Movement Convention in San Bernardino.

By mid-November, I have now caught 25 rabbits. Quail season opened, Papa shot one. Jack and Papa worked hard on well—now down to 45 feet. I began two caps and two coats for Belgian war babies. Finished <u>The Schonberg Colta Family</u>, delightful and inspiring chronicles giving period and life of Luther.

Took my knitting when I drove the goats out, and I knit while I herded. Mother and I went to the Red Cross afternoon, taking clothes old and new for the Belgians. Washed some of my large doll Beth's clothes to give to the Belgian babies. Trapped my 30th rabbit.

DECEMBER

Day before Christmas. I went to town early with Papa to help fill candy boxes for the Sunday school tree. In the afternoon I knitted while out with the goats, and then I helped Aunt Mamie decorate our tree and the house. Later we all went to the Sunday school tree after which Papa, Jack, and I went about town with carolers.

Our first anniversary on December 25, and with it the deep special significance and a richly happy one. We had stockings and the tree and then Jack went to hunt while I helped with dinner. May our happiness grow like this with all the years. We straighten the house. Several of my presents are dear baby things in which I delight.

Digging of the well finished on December 28th. It is 60 feet deep with about 22 feet of water counting that in the side tunnels. We are all glad.

ENTRIES FROM MY JOURNAL 1918

JANUARY

ELSINORE — I did some writing and revising of a story Hylinda called. Jack in one shot at sparrows got 12. He also shot a rabbit.

By mid—January, we heard from the War Department that Jack is in Class 4 and we are thankful! Jack plowed with the mules. Aunt Mamie, Jack, and I went in the evening to hear Major Hendershot. It has been reported that he was only nine years old when he served as a drummer in the Civil War. For years, he has toured the United States recounting Civil War stories. Jack took in the money at the door.

Did some typewriting and reading in W. Gladdens <u>Being a Christian</u> and in McDonald's <u>Malcolm</u>. Rainy day I studied Welsh. Jack surprised us by coming home with the new mule team in the evening. He came from Los Angeles in two days.

Two rabbits in traps, making 41 that I have trapped. I went with mother to Red Cross. Papa and Jack sowed wheat and harrowed it in, while I drove the goats.

I have begun some sorting and packing with Palomar in view. Studied Welsh. Did sewing on baby things. Potatoes and barley planted.

FEBRUARY

I went to Sunday school and church hearing an Anti-Saloon League man. This organization is supposedly the most powerful prohibition lobby in America. I wrote to Jack's people. Hylinda is back from Long Beach, had supper with us. She is doing church work for M. E. Church.

MARCH

Papa and Jack went to see Mr. Langstaff's hill ranch but decided there is too much roadwork required there. Therefore, Papa is planning to make terms with Mr. Hewlett and have the Palomar place back. There have been some failures with the apple crops the last few years and the Hewletts cannot continue to lease it. Papa gave them money so they could move, though they owed him. He had kept waiting and did not want to foreclose.

Packed most of my large trunk, including kitchen utensils, table linens, etc. We keep wondering if Ernest really will enlist. Papa and Mother came home from Long Beach. I think the trade for this place has gone through.

We have now heard that the physician rejected Ernest when he tried to join the Canadian Army. Ernest, born in England, felt the Canadian Army would be an opportunity to serve his former country. Alice and the babies are to come Saturday. I packed while most of the family cleaned the house in the village.

Plans readjusted, as we are not going to Palomar. I began sterilizing sheets and towels for the birth of our baby.

On March 16th, Papa and mother drove very early to San Bernardino to meet Alice and the children. So good to see them! All together now, but Ernest. We enjoyed the children immensely. Junior is the funniest baby, and Dorothy is very merry, and beautiful. They are both dears.

Mother, Papa, and I came down to the village March 21st to a white cottage in the suburbs that we have rented for a month, where I shall be nearer the Dr. I miss Jack.

Washed and mended. Papa took Alice and babies to the ranch, Hylinda staying here. She, mother, and I walked to the hill back of the house, fine view and wildflowers are lovely.

Papa called and Alice and babies came to visit again. Two cards and a letter from my Jack, who stayed at Anaheim Thursday night, then went on to Long Beach and Los Angeles, trying to make deals for Father.

Easter, March 31—Our little Catherine May was born at 3:10 p.m. Oh, such happiness to have her! It is wonderful to be a mother.

APRIL

Our day-old baby seems well and happy. I love the touch of her. Mrs. Ballard, my nurse, had to go so

Ernest, Alice and Dorothy Burley

another nurse, Mrs. Nelson, came. Jack came from Los Angeles, met by the news of his daughter's arrival. I love him more than ever. We decided on the baby's name, Catherine May, Catherine for her Welsh grandmother and May for my mother. I thoroughly like Dr. Shank.

Catherine May is two weeks old. I went to the table for meals today. Papa decided that we really will go to Palomar for Mr. Hewlett has agreed to Papa's last proposition! I feel like a homing pigeon returning to her nest.

I sat in a chair today for the first time since Catherine was born, and it seemed good. I enjoy talking with Mrs. Nelson, the nurse. Papa and Ernest left for Palomar.

Mrs. Nelson left and mother began looking after Catherine and me. Jack came for a few minutes, but he is too busy seeding to stay long. Papa and Ernest came back late. I walked a little about the room, feeling well and stronger. Jack called bringing poppies, wild hyacinths, Indian paintbrushes, owl's ears, baby blue eyes, and other wildflowers!

My blessed baby is sweeter all the time. Now that she is nearly three weeks old, I have begun looking after her altogether at night. I am washing the baby's things now, as I am stronger every day. Elsinore ranch not yet sold as we had hoped.

I wrote Catherine's Welsh grandparents about her. While Jack sat translating a Welsh letter a startling earthquake came. It did damage in San Jacinto and Hemet. Jack and I were alone overnight with the baby, our first real family life.

Jack came by on his way from the ranch to Palomar April 26, and I hated to say goodbye. Catherine has brought us closer together and what she means to us both!

Jack has been away three days, and Catherine went on her first trip, my first in over five weeks. We have left the cottage behind, and have come back out to the ranch.

Yesterday, Papa, mother, Alice, and her children headed for Palomar early in the morning, leaving Aunt Mamie and me alone with the baby. Jack came today to take the cow up. They all spent the night on the grade, Papa walking up most of it.

MAY

We talk of going north, so Alice and Ernest can be at Palomar instead of us. Baby weighs six pounds, five weeks old. Jack is trying to sell things again and got rid of two chickens for a Greek fiesta! He is surely a good salesman. Wish he could sell the ranch by a deal that would go through.

Jack met Sgt. Hicks of the Seaforth Highlanders on the street in Elsinore, stopped to speak of the war. Sgt. Hicks has been on the front 14 months. He and Jack had a fine time talking mutual friends in Vancouver. Sgt. Hicks came out to the ranch in the afternoon, and we all enjoyed them. Catherine gave Sgt. Hicks her first smile.

Jack decided to start on the afternoon of May 9 for Palomar and camp, hoping to go all the way by machine. Later we found out that Jack had a narrow escape in an auto accident on the grade. I tremble and am thankful to God for Jack's life.

About 3 a.m. our expected members of the family came — drove with the team from Palomar. Plans now are that Jack and I are to stay there.

Papa and Aunt Mamie left for Palomar after spending the night in town. Mother stayed there all day packing. Hylinda and I are alone with the baby. I am really learning Bible texts (that Aunt Annie once gave me 15 years ago) while I nurse Catherine. Hylinda walked to town and brought back mail. I had a check for $3. My first money for material accepted, the little Arbor Day pageant printed in "Primary Education." Letter from Wales, they are excited over Catherine's arrival.

Catherine is almost two months old. Busy day, packing books, etc. We surely have too many things for easy moving.

Went to see the doctor in Elsinore on the 27th and saw 800 soldiers with 700 horses, 143rd Regiment, Field Artillery on its way to Los Angeles. I read that the 143rd, based at Camp Kearney, await going to Europe in August.

Hylinda left for Long Beach. Catherine's first trip up the mountain. Despite showers we left with Papa, Mother, baby, and I at about 9 a.m., Passed through cloudbursts then more rainstorms kept Jack from meeting us. We stayed at the Indian rooming house at the reservation. Word arrived at Pala (where Papa planned to meet us with the wagon) that the road washed out.

We stayed two nights in Pala with the Indians. Salvadora (Mrs. Valenzuela) is the Indian who has the rooming house and teaches at the lace school for Indians. We visited yesterday and she really is delightful. Catherine had colic and one of the Indian women rocked her in her arms and hushed her. Her crooning was high with a bit of a weird sound to it.

Catherine is two months old and we have arrived at the apple ranch, The Firs, Palomar. Mr. Hunt brought us to a place near Pauma where Papa got Augustine, another superior Indian (stone deaf) to bring us up the grade. Left the foot of the grade at 4:30 p.m. and surprised the family at 9:30 p.m. The trip was beautiful. It feels good to be here on my mountain after over seven years of absence. I learned of Jack's accident on May 9.

A delight to wake in this beautiful place, the top of the world.

Left—San Luis Rey Mission—The Mission settlements, one-day's ride apart, became reasonable goals when traveling by horse and wagon. Right—Pala Mission

Papa became postmaster in Esther Hewlett's place. The United States government decided I was Welsh when I married Jack, and I could not officially serve as postmaster until he had his citizenship papers. The government classified me as an alien and Catherine therefore considered alien.

Jack has leased all available apple orchards on the mountain to add to the thirteen acres of apples on Papa's ranch.

JUNE

Jack, Aunt Mamie, and I went to Faerie Wood, a great delight. Mr. and Mrs. Salmons called. Jack went to look for trout and heard bees.

I was out of doors with the baby again the next day. While calling on Alice at her camp under the firs where she moved to today, we planted ferns from Faerie Wood.

Our men are still working very hard with ploughing, harrowing, removing weeds of years, planting, etc. I delight in having fresh strawberries and rhubarb. For dessert, we had a green gooseberry pie with war crust (made with barley). The war seems far away.

We also have our own raspberries as well as blackberries. We are getting currants, mulberries, cherries, and corn from Louis Salmons' place. Using rye, barley and oat flour (with wheat) to make waffles (war waffles). There is a constant baking of bread. Mother and I (helped by Aunt Mamie) made quantities of jam.

Washing and ironing are constant jobs. The washer operates by a hand crank. The wringer is also hand operated.

Papa and Mama left with the team for Elsinore June 7, to be gone ten days or so. Alice and I took our children part way to the old Smith-Douglass hotel. Dorothy (age three) helps me wash Catherine's clothes. Jack took a long tramp and brought back delicious brook trout he caught with his hands. Baked barley bread.

Jack began using Miss Maria Frazier's mule. He drove the mules back to Miss Maria's and walked the three miles home, seeing a wild bobcat on the way. I made fresh green gooseberry pie with war crust.

Jack is digging out weeds between the apple trees, getting rid of suckers. It is hard work. Ernest is away working on the road, Alice and babies camping. I enjoy cooking ever so much, though I appreciate Aunt Mamie's help. Lately I made strawberry shortcake, cheese soufflé, barley bread, and bannocks.

I remembered Pomona College commencement, June 17, on my first absence from the whole of it for years. Jack pushed Catherine in her carriage and Aunt Mamie and I followed to the old Cleaver place for cherries to can. Jack began working on telephone line, and brought Mr. Smith and Mr. Cox, who were working with him, to dinner. I hoed weeds from the potatoes.

Jack away all day on June 20th and camped overnight, while working on the telephone line. Ernest and the men continue working on the road at Tin Can Flats, camping overnight there.

Catherine is growing and thriving. Jack gave me a lesson in digging morning glory vines (which he likes me to do for exercise) while Catherine hung in an apple tree in a soapbox swing that Jack made. Jack went for a walk and brought Aunt Mamie iron water and me azaleas.

Mail days Tuesday, Thursday, and Saturday of each week bring some diversion. I welcome it as a time for socializing. There are not many

Jack, second from right, with his road crew—Photo by Robert Asher

gatherings for mountain folks otherwise. The post office is open from noon to one p.m. Representatives of mountain families come to the post office, usually on horseback, with a flour sack or a sugar sack tied to the back of the saddle to hold any mail going or coming for the family.

The post office has always been located at the home of the postmaster, wherever on the mountain that might be. It also serves as the branch library. The residents who first owned and settled the Mack place had constructed a large and well-built barn with a stable at the back. The front portion, entirely separated from the back but under the same roof, serves as a two-room apartment. The post office was located there when we moved onto the property. Once when a government postal inspector came by on his rounds, he was horrified. "It's an insult to the United States government to have a post office in a barn!" he said.

The pay allocated by the postal service to fourth-class postmasters is very low. Income comes chiefly from the value of cancelled stamps on letters mailed. If a dollar's-worth of stamps (on letters and parcels) is purchased and sent out, the postmaster eventually receives a dollar. There is a small additional payment for the sale of money orders. It costs three cents per ounce to mail a letter. I have read that they actually offer airmail service to certain cities for a higher fee. However, it still takes a horse to get the mail up Palomar.

Papa went with Mr. Salmons to help pull up the auto that went off the grade when Jack was providentially saved May 9. As many afternoons as convenient, Mother, Aunt Mamie, Catherine, and I take our mending or sewing up under the trees at Alice's camp.

JULY

On July 2, Papa and Mama left for Elsinore, taking Ernest on his way to Long Beach. Alice and her babies are to sleep by the house. Catherine wears few clothes these warm days. Jack is making a turkey pen in hope of keeping mountain lions away from them. We heard a mountain lion scream on the hill behind the house and have seen one near Faerie Wood. Jack and I had a fine tramp to Boucher's Point, got cherries and wild berries.

Baked bread, rolls, and bannocks and helped get ready for a picnic near Chimney Flats to celebrate July 4th. Alice and children, Aunt Mamie, Jack, and I all enjoyed it. I carried Catherine in my arms. Azaleas lovely! I turned the grindstone for Jack. Catherine and I went with Jack to the east end for corn. We had quite a visit with the Salmons girls. Canned apricots.

On Sunday, we had a beautiful walk with Jack to the Iron Spring in Doane Valley. At sunset went with him to the point after helping doctor the white horse, Boy, "Hooverizing" throughout the house. Miss Maria Frazier called.

Made green apple pie and waffles I invented using half oat and rice flour. Sometimes I use barley and oat flour as in war waffles. Also using rye flour. Constant baking of barley, cornmeal, and wheat bread. Herbert Hoover and the Food Administration have asked American families to save one pound of flour per week. I am doing my part for the war effort. Raspberries are ripe and delicious. We have had a round of rhubarb, strawberries, gooseberries, green apples, blackberries, cherries and lately raspberries. Currants, mulberries, and cherries and corn come from the Salmons' place on the east end of Palomar. Postman had lunch with us.

Papa and Mama left for Elsinore July 17 taking Ernest, Alice, and children on their way to Long Beach to stay. We surely miss them. Marjorie Salmons, now tall, interesting, and capable, came to say that Indians would soon be by to work the road. She stayed to lunch, and Jack went with the Indians to take Ernest's place helping with the roadwork. My Welsh Bible arrived from my Welsh parents. I made an apple pie Jack promised the Indians.

Jack finished working on the road on July 23, and is home to stay. Mother and Papa telephone from Pala on their way home. Jack took Aunt Mamie, Catherine, and I to the east end of Palomar, where we called on the Salmons' family and got currants. Constant baking. Washing and ironing are such exhausting jobs.

Even though it is the last week in July, it is still very cool or cold in the night just now. Mother and I canned seven pints of mixed raspberry and currant jam. Baked bread again. Picked some blackberries. Sent a letter to Wales to thank my parents-in-law for the Welsh Bible and tell them of dried apricots we sent. War news is better these days.

AUGUST

Catherine weighs nine pounds at four months old on August 1. Papa now serving as the postmaster. Jack is cutting props for apple trees and picking apples again.

Jack left early for Elsinore August 2 taking ten boxes of early apples. I hoed up morning glory vines among the apple trees with Catherine in a box hung from a tree. I climbed trees to pick early apples, taking Jack's place in that work.

Catherine likes to be on the porch, seems fond of the hopvines. I picked twelve-fourteen quarts blackberries. Aunt Mamie picked seven quarts of red raspberries. Mother canned twenty pints of berries. Picked berries day after day and dried apples.

Letter and card from Jack on August 8, he is looking after grain, etc. in hot Elsinore, up to 114°. Papa sent down six boxes of apples. Jack's

Salmons girls with Elsie, third from right

hunting license came. Carl Mendenhall asked us all for dinner tomorrow but no Jack or horses. Milton Bailey came with his small son, Steve, asking if Jack could help him soon and if we would spend the winter in his house.

Picked more early apples August 12. Did extra baby's washing. I take her out by wash bench where she enjoys sunflowers. I am studying mutable Welsh consonants while resting. Papa and Mother went to the Fraziers and got two pigs.

Milton, wife, and son Steve called on August 16th. Jack and I walked to Boucher's. Happy tramp. Got "Palomar Giants"—extremely large apples to show. Jack and Papa cut and put up props for apple trees when they can find time.

On August 25, I helped Jack pick nine boxes, nearly all from one apple tree (not packed).

Jack and I went to Faerie Wood and on the way followed bees and found deer tracks. The glorious lilacs and lemon lilies found on my favorite portion of the land, that I named Faerie Wood, requires a walk across from the road from the farmhouse. It is a secluded and delightful hideaway.

Election Day, Tuesday, August 27th. Our post office served as the polls. I helped Papa with mail.

Wednesday, just after supper Mr. Davis phoned the dreadful news of Miss Maria Frazier's death Sunday. I remember the first time Alice and I met Miss Lizzie Frazier. We had mounted the same horse, gone for a ride of exploration, and stopped at their house. Miss Lizzie was so excited at having callers and meeting new neighbors that she questioned us so fast she could not wait for answers. "You're really a family? Where'd you come from?"

The Frazier sisters lived alone. They were very interesting, fine, and independent women. Miss Maria and Miss Lizzie Frazier had been seamstresses that had tired of city life. They chose Palomar Mountain because they wanted something more primitive. For a little while, Miss Lizzie carried the mail on horseback. She was one of the first mail carriers. Maria and Lizzie had cattle, cut their own wood, and took care of their own affairs. They fit the description of old maids. Miss Maria was the one who did all the work and took care of Miss Lizzie, who by then had become bedfast.

On August 29, I looked after mail alone. Jack came in afternoon after helping make coffin, dig grave, burial terrible due to circumstances. Miss Lizzie is bearing up wonderfully. Jack related the story to us. Miss Maria had died suddenly of a heart attack while in bed, and Miss Lizzie managed to crawl out of the house and opened the gates to the corral somehow to let the cattle out. It was four days before anyone came to check on them. Miss Lizzie sat in a chair in the yard waiting for help. Jack said that Miss Lizzie was poised, dignified and unshaken by the experience. The coroner had come up the mountain but could not locate where the Frazier sisters lived. Jack and the men on the mountain went down and buried Miss Maria. Since she had been dead four days, it was necessary to dig a large hole, carry her body out with the mattress and bury her.

The people living on Palomar are strong, self-sufficient and sometimes eccentric individuals. I am proud to be a part of them as I watch them take on tasks to assist each other.

Mrs. Bailey phoned after supper about fire in woods, started by lightning. Jack helped fight it all evening. Fire-fighting implements are stored at our ranch.

SEPTEMBER

Bought two pigs (one hundred-sixty-one pounds) from Milton Bailey on September 3rd. Jack and I had the post office work. We packed a box of pears and peaches and sent it for Ernest's birthday. Mrs. Davis brought large piece of veal from the Mendenhalls.

Jack sold apples to Mr. Plummer, $2.65 a hundred, delivered to the foot of grade. I put baby Catherine on the ground while I picked apples. Later, I left Catherine in an apple box while I hoed up pesty wild morning glory vines.

Mid-September and Mr. Frazier, a whimsical, jolly old Illinois farmer began visiting us between business trips.

Sunday- Little morning service. All of us singing together with the Fraziers added much to the family prayer time.

Hylinda started down the mountain with a bicycle. She phoned later from Pala. Helped Miss Lizzie Frazier September 18 with sewing and pressing and writing, the last was an epitaph for her sister.

The Fraziers left the next day, Clinton Bailey coming for them by machine. The good news is that the Allies WIN splendidly, America going ahead. Papa went to the Frazier place bringing back furniture he and Jack are to sell for Miss Lizzie. Wrote a lullaby after trying it out on Catherine. Papa went by horseback to try to get Indians as apple pickers.

By September 24, we began picking regular crop. Picked about fifty lug boxes. Jack went down the grade for more apple boxes. He stayed at Nate's the next night. Got home at 9 a.m. Mr. Hill and Mr. Hewlett helping us pick. I put Catherine on ground in the orchard again while I picked. Helped put out plums to dry.

Last day in September and I worked all day on post office quarterly reports. Four Indians working here now. Post office Inspector came, so I rejoiced in the fact that I had already been doing the straightening. Two stray boys and inspector for dinner besides usual crowd. Jack cleaned the apple cider press. Aunt Mamie takes care of Catherine during mail time hours.

OCTOBER

Jack took down fifty-two boxes of apples and brought back empty boxes. Apples piled high under the firs.

A week later—Sadie and I picked up apples the wind had blown down.

Made some cider. Wish mother were not so busy cooking for Indians, and that I could do more. I made grape juice (fresh) in the cider press.

Sent pudding ingredients to Wales. Canned three quarts grape juice. The Hewletts came in the afternoon, and we had a Sunday service. Walked down to Lower Doane and found twenty kinds of wildflowers on the way, good for mid-October.

Oct. 29—I will certainly never forget Milton Bailey's kindness on this desperate occasion during this our first year of Jack running the ranch. Jack suddenly had a terrible hemorrhage from a previously undiagnosed stomach ulcer, and had to see a doctor as soon as possible. My parents were with us, but since Jack's accident on the grade, there was temporarily no car in the family. An SOS to Milton brought him over at once, and he drove us to Elsinore where we rented a cottage for several weeks, to be near our friend, Dr. Shank. There is a dreadful flu epidemic going on, and the doctors said there was no use considering the Riverside Hospital, which was overflowing into the halls. Jack could scarcely sit up, and on the way down, I sat in dread with my seven-month-old baby in my arms. Milton drove with solicitous care, not to start another hemorrhage with unnecessary jolting on bad roads, yet as fast as he dared to reach the doctor. We were deeply grateful. We took one of the Keck cottages. Dr. Shank says Jack must not eat today and must be still.

Oct. 30—Today Jack is allowed a glass of milk every two hours and bits of ice. I try not to worry too much. He is very patient.

Oct. 31—Staying busy as nurse and nursemaid. Jack remains brave and patient. As Jack is so weak that it bothers him terribly when Catherine cries, I now take her to town every time I go.

Five days after our harrowing scare Jack is coming on well and may now have three eggs a day beaten and mixed with milk. He suffers little now.

The doctor made a long social call last night. He said Jack might get up today. So he was dressed and sat in a chair.

NOVEMBER

Nov. 7—Premature news of peace made wild celebration.

On the 10th, I woke feeling miserable and grippy. Half afraid my bad cold is Spanish Influenza now raging. We sent a note to Dr. Shank who came and prescribed for us all. Jack may now have purees, etc. So glad he is so much better.

By the next day, Jack was well enough that he now goes to the village Main Street several times a day, and does errands. It is good he is able to be out now. <u>Peace declared!!!</u> The world thanks God. Went downtown for afternoon celebration.

Nov. 13—I feel much better, more able to look after my family, and am grateful. The Spanish flu has at last really come to Elsinore. Grateful too for our escape so far (unless it is what I have been having). Jack went to the Hot Springs for a Sulphur bath.

Nov. 19—Today Jack had his first meal for three weeks, tea and toast, split pea puree, and coddled egg. Rainy weather. Yesterday washed my hair with tar soap and began putting herbicide on it, as it is coming out. Catherine pulls out handfuls!

Mr. Hunt phoned home and found roads too bad, too much rain for us to go up Thursday. We went with Mr. Hunt about the lake.

By Thanksgiving, we were back on Palomar with snow on the ground. Had fifteen stuffed roasted quail substituted for the expected Thanksgiving turkey.

I failed to keep a journal for the rest of 1918. As I recall, it was an extremely busy apple season with many workers picking, sorting, packing, drying and hauling apples. Of course, we women were kept very busy helping them as well as providing three meals a day for the apple crew.

6

Following Mountain Ways 1919

Mountain Blessing
By Elsie Roberts

I followed mountain ways.
Wild lilacs touched my face,
The fern fronds bent in grace,
And in the fire, the wind sang ancient lays.
So to the crest I came,
Where richest fancies flame,
And Beauty holds a pageant all the days.
Bright flowers wave in the breeze,
And down across the trees
The vales and hills reach to the sea's blue haze.
But lo! Over all there lay,
Touched with a mystic light,
The drifted cloud banks—white,
Exquisite, visible silence, the snow of May.
The distant sea was gone,
The heights and depths were one,
Holy and boundless calm at the close of the day.
Through all Nature the vast hush stole,
And it brought to my troubled soul
The Peace of God, that nothing can take away.

ENTRIES FROM MY JOURNAL 1919

JANUARY

New Year's Day—Palomar Mountain—A busy happy day. Jack went hunting, getting two gray squirrels and six quail. I helped clean the latter, washed clothes, and made out the post office quarterly reports. Catherine likes animals.

An Indian, Peter Grand, came back bringing teams and wagon last night. Today, he and Jack each took two loads of apples to the saddle (the low point between two hills, just above Nate's cabin) today, first time by sleds, then wagon. Snow is melting fast. Post office work, catalog shopping, cleaning our bedroom took my day.

Several days have passed since my last entry. I accomplished general housework, mending and ironing. Studied Welsh while cutting apples for dryer, meanwhile being on the porch giving Catherine her fresh air while she slept. I cannot leave her alone now because of the wild pigs!

Thermometer went to 48 degrees today. Baked eight loaves of bread I started last night. Did some other cooking for Sunday. Post office day again.

Jack, Elsie and Catherine at Planwydd

Sunday—Jack drove Aunt Mamie, Catherine, and me to the deserted house where the Hewletts had lived at Silvercrest. Papa bought their furniture, etc. Fun looking over things they left. The Indians sang with us in the afternoon.

At the end of the week, Papa left for Pala, and Pete took apples down the grade; while

Jack went down to mend telephone line, gone all day. Catherine said "Teddy" fairly plainly for her Teddy Bear—first undisputed word! We washed clothes, dried apples, etc.

The next day Jack did not feel so well after the jolting going down the hill yesterday. Papa got back from Pala. Jack went to the Hills to milk cows late after supper.

Jack went twice more to the Hills to milk their cows while Mr. Hill is away. I helped make cider, mended old trousers. I did some mail order shopping, made two buckets of cider, helped carry in wood, and started the ram to provide water for the house, etc. Water on the apple ranch comes piped from the spring to a tank near our home. A device called a hydraulic ram accomplishes this task. The ram transfers the water from the pond across the road, up the hill and into the storage tank for the house. We listen for the ram, and when it becomes silent, we go to it and operate a valve with our foot to restart it. Papa piped water into the house, but an outhouse is still in use.

We have a forest fire on the mountain but it is not as bad today as it was yesterday and the day before. Jack worked on the telephone line again and Modesto worked on the road while Pete took another load of apples down.

Roast Squirrel. ✓   Mr. David Swain.

Clean + season + dip in flour.
Brown in fat in frying pan.
Add water + put in baking pan
with onions, + potatoes if desired.
Bake about 1½ hrs., with cover on pan.

Squirrel + Quail Pie. ✓

Stew + cut squirrel (+ quail) into pieces;
add potatoes cut rather small + sliced onions.
Season to taste. Bake with crust.

I made nine loaves of bread and a pan of rolls, also made ice cream frozen with snow.

I put the library books in order (part of my post office job) and made out a library report. Helped Jack a little with apples, cooked, etc.

On Sunday Jack, Catherine, Aunt Mamie, and I went again to Silvercrest, a beautiful drive through the woods. Brought home more magazines, etc. A party of Elsinore people came up, the Grahams and Bohanans. Modesto and Peter Grand, the two Indians hauling and packing apples, joined us singing hymns and Catherine sang, too. Hylinda played the little school house organ, as the family piano was not brought up the grade.

I have special help or easy dinners on mail days. Made five loaves of bread and twenty rolls. Now using homemade or liquid yeast instead of the dry. Jack left unexpectedly for San Diego with the carrier, as our apple arrangements need care. I miss him!

With help from Hylinda and Aunt Mamie, we got dinner for Mr. Kiefer, two other men and two boys who came for some apples. Mr. K. gave us a fine large piece of meat in pay! Made pies and turnovers. The magazines for the library have begun to come, a little more work, but well worth it.

Jack has been gone two days, and I surely miss him. Did a family washing, cooked, helped a little sorting apples and started orange marmalade. Glorious weather, bright, even warm.

Jack came home late, walking up the grade, seven miles. Such a joy to have him back. I did extra cleaning, etc. with post office work and cooking. Jack's new apple arrangements are good.

Sunday—Papa, Aunt Mamie, and I drove the pigs to an acorn ground on top of the ridge, far along. Beautiful views the pigs cannot appreciate! We talked, read, and rested later. All of us walked with Jack to Silvercrest.

Fog and rain so Pete and Modesto left. Besides, Modesto came back from the reservation last night with mumps. Washed, mended, and cooked since I am the cook still except for breakfasts. Wrote my "Palomar Paragraphs" sent weekly to Escondido and Oceanside newspapers!

Jack went down the grade with a load of apples again, bringing up hay. Mrs. Davis brought me some of her orange marmalade; it is better than mine.

My birthday—January 22. A busy birthday with baby-clothes washed, some mending done, etc. Froze ice cream with snow and made a white cake. Aunt Mamie and I are having our dinner together. Jack hauled apples again and brought me flowers at night.

Had a fine lot of mail, some of it for my birthday. Catherine was especially jolly. Drove hogs to live oaks. Jack does not feel so well after three days on the grade. Beautiful weather for January.

I heard from Mrs. Hurst of Karl's death, for he bravely gave his life for his country on October 18. I cannot realize it. It seems just the other day that Karl and I met in Arizona when I taught in Cornville. He imagined he was in love with me and asked me to marry him. He was a fine man and I enjoyed his friendship, but I desired a man who loved books. When the war started, Karl enlisted in the Army. I was proud of him. Mrs. Hurst wrote that Karl died from poison gas in France. My heart aches with this sad news.

Sunday—Mrs. Shank and I rode horseback almost to Mrs. Martin's while Jack took Doctor Shank and his son to Palomar Hotel. We four without Robert walked to Boucher's and saw the sunset there. Sang hymns in the evening.

Today Mrs. Shank and Robert helped me drive the pigs to pasture. I cooked, etc. In the afternoon, we coasted on left over snow at this end of Alice's Valley. We went to Inspiration Point just after sunset. From that view, we could see Catalina Island across the glistening Pacific.

A horse kicked our hired man, Pete, last night so Jack went with him to La Jolla Indian Reservation and arranged for Tony to come up. Despite the fog Jack, mother, and I packed the last of the apples (with some extras saved). Papa took down one load, Tony another. They seem to keep rather well having lasted in storage for seven months. We keep them from touching each other by using hay or newspaper.

The snow began today, catching Tony before he got back from hauling. Jack worked at taking down the tent house bought from the Hewletts at Silvercrest. Weather was bad all day.

FEBRUARY

Yesterday Jack went in a snowstorm for the old mare, to Fraziers' place. I am still the cook. The snow is still falling, though not steadily, twelve and a half inches of it now. Our old mare got down and had to be shot.

After four days of snowing, we have glorious snow scenes. I took a number of pictures. The sky is a most wonderful deep blue and branches laden with snow.

Jack went far down on old grade to get a mare from Fraziers' pasture, but it was so far down and snow so deep he did not go far enough. Mr. Jolly, the mail carrier, is to bring it up Saturday.

I finished C's first rompers, made from a gray silky finish-shirt of Jack's, trimmed with red. Jack took Catherine and me to Silvercrest, for a fine sleigh ride. We are planning, he and I, to rent the old Smith-Douglas Hotel place.

February 10—A peculiar looking tramp appeared today, despite snow on ground, with an ax on his shoulder and began to work for us as a woodchopper. William Oliver said he was a professional woodcutter, and wouldn't we like him to cut some for us? Wood is our only fuel for heating

The family on a sleigh ride

and cooking, so although we had already a great stack just the length for either a big kitchen range or the heating stove in the dining room, we were always glad to have more ready, cut the proper length. Jack left and went down to Lone Fir for wagon.

Papa, Mother, and Hylinda are getting ready to start for Long Beach tomorrow.

We have another storm, so the family is still here, unable to travel as planned.

Papa, Mother and Hylinda left with team and a light wagon bound for Long Beach. Jack and the woodcutter went to the snow line to help dig out drifts, etc.

I made apple butter, nine pints. I did quite a washing in honor of the clear day. Jack looked after the mail.

This has been an exciting week! Jack and woodcutter killed a pig. In the afternoon, Jack had planned to butcher our one hog but he and the newcomer and perhaps others had a great deal of trouble trying to catch it. Finally, in disgust he shot it. Then the sharp butcher knives flew. I baked bread. The woodcutter was using his ax and when it was lunchtime, I fed him at a table in the kitchen. He looked up at me with a sort of leer and asked, "Aren't you going to sit down and eat with me?" I refused and he ate alone. I was frying hog meat and at the same time baking bread in the big wood range, when at dusk there came a knock at the door. Aunt Mamie with baby Catherine in her arms opened the door. Aunt Mamie said afterward, she almost dropped the baby. Two big uniformed men stood there. The Sheriff of Santa Ana then arrested our woodcutter as a murderer!!! Another sheriff and Mr. Keith of Elsinore came, too. Got dinner for them all and felt so odd serving the murderer.

As hospitality was somewhat obligatory on the mountain those days, I did not sit with the men at dinner. Jack, the two sheriffs and their prisoner, whose face was then a deep red said little or nothing, but every time I passed about the tables serving them, I had the feeling that man might suddenly reach out and grab me. Fortunately, we could give the Sheriffs and the man a place to sleep that was not in the house. Mr. Mack, the first owner of the place, had built a large barn and stable. The walls separated the stable from the front two rooms in the barn.

The next day the officers left with their prisoner and Mr. Keith after breakfast. We got the whole story from Papa when he returned. They had gone down the mountain and Papa went into a barbershop for service. The barber, who knew him, said, "Did you see anything of that murderer who was spotted climbing the Palomar grade with an ax on his shoulder?"

Papa had seen a man in the yard with an ax. The barber further told him the word was that the man had a tattoo on his wrist. My father had noticed that identification and seemed certain it was he, and the two sheriffs started for the mountain. I wrote up the story for Escondido and Oceanside newspapers. We packed apples to send to friends. Mr. & Mrs. Salmons came in from post office for lunch.

Santa Ana Daily Register Newspaper February 17, 1919

Chopping Wood Oliver Taken Upon Top of Smith Mountain

Murderer remembers nothing of escape, asks if he hurt anyone.

William Oliver, murderer, who escaped from the County hospital January 30, was returned to jail Saturday evening at 6:30 p.m. He was taken into custody Friday evening at the top of Smith Mountain, where he was at work chopping wood. He made no resistance. Almost his first question was as to whether or not he had hurt anyone in getting away. He says his mind was a blank for some days while he was in jail until he recovered his senses somewhere in the foothills.

Oliver was in the county jail here in January awaiting trial on a charge of murdering Joe Morales, a fisherman, at Anaheim landing on November 6. He shot Morales following a quarrel because Morales abused Oliver's pet cat.

In jail, he developed what appeared to be signs of insanity. He feared that Mexicans were at his cell door awaiting the chance to kill him. That he might be observed he was transferred to the County hospital. There, on the night of January 30, he used a sidebar of an iron bed to beat a hole through the cell wall and out of this hole he escaped.

On February 9, Tony Keith of Elsinore reported that he had seen a man on Smith Mountain who fitted Oliver's description. Motorcycle officers Ballard and Stewart went to the Canyon, but returned when they were satisfied that Oliver had gone over the mountain to Warners' ranch.

But Oliver did not go on to Warner's ranch. He stopped at the Hayes' and Roberts' ranch at the very top of the mountain. There is the little post office called Nellie, located in the ranch barn, and there are two or three buildings where summer boarders sleep. Hayes and his son-in-law have an apple orchard, and it was in this orchard that Oliver got the job chopping wood. He arrived there last Monday and there were 18 inches of snow. He was given a bed in the post office, and was eating at the table with the family.

A few days ago, Mr. and Mrs. Hayes drove down off the mountain on their way to Long Beach for a visit. Arriving at Elsinore they first heard that it was supposed that there was an escaped murderer, probably insane, somewhere on Smith Mountain. From the description, he had no doubt that the man chopping wood at Nellie was Oliver. Word was sent by telephone to Santa Ana, and Thursday night Under-Sheriff Iman, Ballard and Keith approached him.

"Hello Bill," said Under Sheriff Iman.

"Hello Jack," responded Oliver.

"How are you feeling Bill?"

"Pretty bad," said Oliver, "but I can tell you better if you'll tell me something." His voice trembled and tears were close to the surface.

"What is it?"

"I've been worrying for thinking I might have hurt someone. Did I hurt anyone getting away? I don't know how I got away; did I hurt anyone?"

"No you didn't hurt anybody at all, Bill."

Oliver gave a great sigh of relief and his face brightened up, and he smiled as though a great load had been lifted from his mind. "I didn't know," he said. "The last I remember was when I was in jail. Where did I get these clothes? These ain't my clothes, Jack." He opened his shirt and held his fingers on the pajamas, which with a pair of socks, was all he had on when he broke out of the hospital.

Iman told the man what had occurred. "And after we lost your tracks we don't know where you went," said Iman.

"I don't know either," said Oliver. "When I came to, I was walking in the foothills somewhere. I was barefooted and didn't have anything on but these pajamas. My legs were cut and scratched up, and I was cold and nearly starving. First, I thought I'd lay down and die. I was afraid I'd hurt somebody breaking out of jail. Then I decided to go on. Finally, I came to a cabin where there was an old prospector, and I told him some kind of story, I don't know what. He gave me something to eat, these old clothes, and these rubber boots. I just kept going. Over at Elsinore, I got some blankets I had left there in November and then I went on. I was afraid that I had killed somebody, and so I kept going. I worked in this country 16 years ago so I came down here."

"You'd better put down that ax," said Iman.

"Jack, I wouldn't hurt you for anything in the world."

"I know you wouldn't, but I think you better put it down." Oliver obeyed him and returned to the house with the three men.

Their explanations were soon made and Mr. and Mrs. Roberts, hospitable in the extreme, made provisions for the overnight stay. The visitors were tired and hungry. Climbing hills and walking through snow raised an appetite. The supper that was served will never be forgotten. Roberts and Oliver had killed a pig that day, and pork without limit and apple cider fresh from the press were served.

Friday night Iman and Ballard took turns staying up, Oliver slept. Saturday the trip to Santa Anna was made. Oliver told Iman and Ballard that years ago he was a cowboy in Texas. He was breaking horses one year when he was kicked in the head by a horse. The silver plate was put in to piece out his skull. About a year later, he had a spell of insanity, and he came to his senses in an asylum somewhere in Delaware or Massachusetts, a part of the world he had never known. After recovering his senses, he went out west. That was 16 years ago, he said. That he has intermittent spells of insanity due to being kicked in the head by a horse when he was a cowboy in Texas nearly 20 years ago is the story told by William Oliver.

We finished another batch of apple butter. I washed seven sheets and many other things with Jack turning machine and wringer. Jack piled apples on ground and painted kitchen ceiling. Fog and rain.

It snowed 1 ½ inches during the night. Mrs. Salmons and later Mrs. Hill called. Baked bread and partly papered the kitchen. I put the pork in brine to be cured and canned quarts of roast pork. Modesto came up and Jack and Julian took down the fence the Hewletts had left at the Smith-Douglas place.

Did some extra post office work. Baked eight loaves of bread, some rolls, and made a raisin pie and extra crusts. We filled the apple dryer. Did further straightening in the kitchen, which looks inviting now.

The first bright day for a long time. Did some ironing, cleaning and mending, and cut up apples for the dryer again. Mail day, I helped Jack with post office work. Took Catherine out in the funny little two-wheeled wagon made of a box and took pictures of her in it and on a sled. On Saturday night, it snowed three inches. On Sunday, we all sat around by the fire and read library books. Too bad we cannot go to church. The next day it was chiefly clear. I made lemon cheese and one scrapbook for hospital children.

Made bread again. The Indians eat amazing amounts of it. Jack mended the Frazier clock and cleaned the typewriter thoroughly

Letter arrived from Jack's father and mother on the Welsh day of celebration, Dydd Santes Dwynwen—celebrating love, much like Valentine's Day It has now been fifteen years since Jack last saw his parents. I try to imagine what it must feel like, since he is their only child. They are eager to have us come over, and we long to go to Wales to see them. Jack went to the Frazier place. Aunt Mamie and I took Catherine up on hill after cones.

On Sunday, made raisin pie, roasted pork, etc. Fog as usual in afternoon. Aunt Mamie and I took Catherine to Faerie Wood, lovely there as always.

The next day despite fog and rain, Jack and Modesto went down the grade to the river to mend telephone line. Jack brought back lovely wild flowers to our snow. The flowers were shooting stars, paintbrush, lupines, peonies, everlasting, navitas, etc.

MARCH

Jack weighed Catherine and she is now sixteen pounds, thirteen oz. at eleven months. Aunt Mamie and I took Catherine out in the little wagon for there was beautiful sunshine. I took advantage of fine day by doing a big washing with extras. Phone is okay Jack pruned fifty-seven apple trees.

Took Catherine out again in her two-wheeled box-cart again and she loves it. Aunt Mamie and I cut up apples for apple butter and the dryer. Jack pruned and Aunt Mamie and I sewed. Catherine began to wear the Western country small-child costume: blue denim coveralls trimmed with turkey red.

I sent Edna a box of apples. Baked eight loaves of bread as the Indians are expected tomorrow. Jack stays busy pruning, but has finished the worst trees.

Mrs. Hill, who was on stage for years, called and talked very entertainingly of literary lights in New York, etc.

Sunday—A beautiful day of sunshine but there is still a great deal of snow between here and Silvercrest. Windy as the month suggests. Jack, Aunt

Mamie, and Catherine in the little cart, the dog, the cow and I went there this morning. Catherine fretted more than usual, poor mite. I put up kitchen curtains, Jack pruned.

Modesto came late last night, so began boarding with three meals today. Jack has now pruned at least 220 apple trees and is burning stumps, too. Aunt Mamie and I went to call on Mrs. Hill at the new place (Clark Cleaver's old ranch) where they stay daytimes a good deal. We took Catherine in the little cart.

Modesto took a load of apples down to the river. Prepared nine more meals for him. Jack pruned forty more trees. I washed and made a cake and pies. I took Catherine out to the orchard to see Jack.

Heavy fog turned into snow. I made hot cocoa for the mail carrier. It has become deep snow—thirteen inches of it. Beautiful, but hard on Jack's plans. Snow fell until night, then clear moonlight. Made bread, cleaned my room. Poor Cadi's (Catherine's) teeth seem to bother her.

Mid-March and it is cold. Mr. Jolly late with mail because of high river. Cocoa for him again.

Hard to believe this is just a day later. Catherine and I spent about two hours on the porch. Really warm! Modesto back from hauling alone as Pete went to Pala for better horses.

Now Fog has turned to snow. When Jack gave us (and Indians) a concert, Catherine beat time with her foot and waved her arms and body in joy.

More stormy, so that the Indians left for home, taking a load of apples on their way. Gave the mail carrier hot soup and cocoa. Jack, Aunt Mamie, and I read a good deal!

Fourth day to remain stormy with the snow keeping at it rather steadily. Between the 14th & 21st of March inclusively twenty-three inches of snow fell. Soup and cocoa for the mail carrier again as he came in the snowstorm. Jack and I talk of living a gypsy life later.

Sunday—Aunt Mamie reads a Bible chapter aloud to us every evening. Jack reads a great deal during these slow winter days.

Some sunshine. Washed clothes. Aunt Mamie and I filled the apple dryer. Indians left with a lunch for several days that I prepared for them. I baked nine loaves of bread, three pies and cooked pork.

Baked bread, but only five loaves. Jack went down almost to Tin Can Flats to mend the phone line. Then mother called up from Pala on way home. Jack went to Doane Valley for iron water. Later Jack decided to go down for his business trip with Mr. Jolly, so he will be going to San Diego tonight.

Sunday—Mr. and Mrs. Swartz of L.A. called. They are walking with blankets on their backs for a vacation and a rest. I took Catherine out on Inspiration Point and stayed there with her for hours. Missed Jack. Mr. Fink came to dinner. Poor Winbert Fink. He lives in a cabin back beyond Mendenhall Valley in a very isolated area. He advertised for a mail order bride and when the woman arrived, she brought a formal wedding gown, a number of sheer blouses and other fashionable attire. I guess she thought if she was going to live in Southern California she should be dressed for resort living. I do not think she liked living on the back of beyond with her nearest neighbors about two miles away. Anyway, she did not stay long. We have tried to befriend him.

Jack telephoned from San Diego that he has bought a car, an Overland. March 31st and our dear baby Catherine is a year old. I had to work on post office monthly and quarterly reports but we took turns pulling her in her cart. She liked her cake. We received a fine package from Wales. I finished weather bureau report and looked over library books, making out quarterly report of circulation.

APRIL

Papa, Mother, Aunt Mamie, and I went to the east end (taking Catherine of course); had a picnic lunch, and then we women called on Miss Hodgie while Papa got about 100 currant bushes.

Jack phoned before leaving San Diego for L.A. I did my family washing, and we all sorted apples with Catherine outside in her pen.

Papa left with the team for Pala. We cleaned house. Mrs. Hill came for lunch and went to Faerie Wood with me. We both enjoyed it. I gathered branches, moss, cones and ferns to send to Edna who has tuberculosis.

Sent some apples to Hotel Westminster, Los Angeles, to Jack and the greenery to Edna. Took Catherine for a ride in her cart and did some cooking. Papa came with Mr. Castle, a discharged soldier that Jack hired to work here.

Sunday—Played Welsh hymns, read in Welsh Bible, looked over some of my poems. I took Catherine in my arms to Chimney Flats and she delighted in it.

Telephone line mended by Mr. Castle. Wet weather. Near sunset, I went over to Silvercrest. From there we can see to the coast. Marvelous effects of cloud and fog in the view below. Went through the jungle to the lower garden there for chard and enjoyed the walk.

A glorious spring day. Did a washing with extras, blankets, etc. Then Catherine and I went to the Hills with Papa to get strawberry plants, we got 700. Catherine put dirt and stones in her mouth and was very happy. Said "pitty" when I called buttercups that.

Two good letters from Jack. He was to see about his naturalization papers.

He was also working hopefully on timber question. We all helped with the planting of the strawberries. Mr. Castle is plowing the orchard and preparing the place for currants.

Did a lot of extra ironing. We put Catherine in her pen by kitchen door, outside. I am cook of course. Felt earthquake 2:15 a.m.

Extra cooking. I helped Papa plant onion sets and helped Catherine plant marigold seeds! Wrote five cards asking for more catalogs, Wanamakers, Franklin Simon, Bentinque Bellas, and Hess & Ville de Paris.

Catherine's protective pen.

Sunday—Aunt Mamie and I climbed the ridge and found wild flowers. In the afternoon Mother, Catherine, and I went down to Doane Trail. Catherine loves the out-of-doors. Mother made Catherine a quaint sunbonnet. I learned part of the Lord's Prayer in Welsh.

Papa left for Pala to meet Jack. He gave Papa a lesson in running our new Overland. Made pies for them before I had breakfast. Then made more before supper for two men from surveying party. They stayed overnight. Mr. Theodore Bailey called.

Cleaned our room and living room, cooked in the morning. Then Jack came with Papa about noon. Surely good to have him back! He had encouraging news about his health and his business.

Mid-April and we went to Chimney Flats for snow and made ice cream. Ironed and mended. Took Catherine out to orchard where Jack was pruning and sowing clover. The clover helps combat other weeds and attracts bees that aid in pollination.

Cooking seems to take a large part of my time! I do grow weary of the constant need to cook for all the hired men. Got some things ready for the mail. Mother is going to look after the post office more than I do now.

Good Friday—Made hot cross buns. Went to Chimney Flats for snow to cool the gelatin. The barley we planted last week is coming up. I helped mother sort apples, wrote some, took Catherine to Jack in the orchard, and visited with him there. I planted red currant bushes. Jack and Mr. Castle finished planting the clover in the orchard across the road. Catherine and I went with Papa and Mr. Castle to Silvercrest for a load, collecting what remained from things Papa purchased from Hewletts.

Easter Sunday—Jack and I had a beautiful tramp into Doane Valley. Found many blue violets. This is Catherine's second Easter! She is very dear and loving. How we love her! Rhubarb pie.

I colored an egg orange with onionskins and mother colored another red for Catherine. She immediately knocked them together. I took her out to where Jack and Mr. Castle were planting potatoes.

Saturday—Mr. Castle left in storm with Mr. Jolly. Snow, hail, etc. We had Mr. Jolly in for hot dinner. Mrs. Davis called, having walked to collect mail through the storm.

Sunday—Very foggy but took Catherine out for rides several times, as she begs for "bye-bye." Jack and I had short walk through lilacs where snow looked like winter still.

Jack planted alfalfa seeds. I made pies and turnovers for Uncle Nate and for Jack on his trips, and for us. All the mountain folk seem to be good about taking food to Uncle Nate when going down or up the grade. Jack left in early afternoon with teams for Pala, for feed, etc. We worked on hop vines and our wildflower bed.

Jack came in late this afternoon with many supplies, including treats of fresh peas and strawberries and candy. We began keeping accounts.

I washed and used soap dye on clothes. I wrote a little. Jack is working very hard hauling brush from the orchard. Apple blossoms are beautiful now. Catherine pulls her sleeve nowadays to show she wants coat on for "bye-bye" as she calls going out or riding in her cart.

MAY

First of May and I planted some sweet pea seeds. Aunt Mamie and I went to Faerie Wood for ferns while mother took care of Catherine. Many flowers are out, lavender lilacs, purple peas, beautiful. Papa, mother, Catherine, and I went to the Hargraves' place where Papa saw Mr. H. about listing his place. Made bread.

Catherine has learned to cluck as Grandpa does to the horses. Busy day, I swept and mopped. Papa and Mama took Catherine on a drive to Silvercrest. Jack planted alfalfa seed sent by our congressman. I made pies, etc. for Sunday.

Sunday—Early breakfast then Jack took Aunt Mamie, Catherine, and me to Boucher. The orchard there is a marvel of bloom, much more than ours. I walked to Inspiration Point and the south plateau below, tried to kill a snake there.

We planted some soybeans near the walnut tree. Jack is still doing hard work plowing, etc., but nearly through with that sort of work.

We left Catherine with her grandparents, and Aunt Mamie, Jack, and I drove to Pala, going to Elsinore from there in the fine new Overland. It goes splendidly.

The next day I shopped and lunched with Jack, then came on to Pala with him, to stay overnight with Salvadora Valenzuelas.

We got up before four and Jack harnessed and finished packing the wagon in the dark. Had breakfast at the foot of the grade and reached home 2:20 p.m. So very glad to see my baby again. She stood alone a minute. Catherine is so dear. She sniffs now when she sees a flower and wants to smell it. She creeps all about. She wears her little rompers, pulls herself up by the side of her pen, and takes steps. She is quite plump and has a good deal of color. Her hands are quite brown, and her wrists also from being out of doors so much, that it looks as if she has on tan clothes. She is a very loving baby, will put her arms around my neck, and put her dear little face against mine. She is good with Mama or with Aunt Mamie in the daytime, but when the shades of night come down, then she wants me to put her to bed and cuddle her up in her own fashion. Jack cut her hair yesterday, straight around, and she does look so cute with bangs. She looks a good deal like Jack. He feeds her at the table.

Mrs. Martin came for overnight, and then the Danes and Thompsons with three infants came to camp. We persuaded the women and children to take the living room.

More library work done today. Mr. Elmore telephoned Jack that work on the road was ready to begin. I looked up extra socks for him. Living this life on our mountain, something always needs fixing.

I helped Jack get ready to go down to work on the road, then mother, Catherine and I drove him down almost to Uncle Nate's cabin.

Papa planted Sudan grass. Miss Burgess is staying on with us, and helped me very much by advising as to altering my old blue silk. It seems funny to have Mama and Papa living in a cotton tent house nearby.

Jack has been away working on the road for three days, and I drove down below Tin Can Flats and brought him back. It was late when we got home. I made six pies for Jack to take down to the men working on the road. We had some frost last night, but it did not hurt things. The yellow roses are blooming, and full of buds.

Sunday—Jack drove Catherine and me down the mountain in the roadwork wagon with pulley brake, horse, mule tied behind, and the mule following. The Shank family joined us at the road camp and I got dinner for all of us. The Shanks took us to their home in Elsinore in their sedan. We are going to L.A. tomorrow to do some shopping. Papa and Mama joined us in Elsinore.

I left Elsinore with Catherine and Mrs. Shank and her children in their new Ford Sedan. Papa and Mother left for Palomar with a crib I bought for Catherine.

I shopped in L.A., though hard with Catherine along. I splurged on a dress (voile) and shoes for myself, etc.

JUNE

Sunday—Stopping in Pasadena for church on our way to Elsinore.

In Elsinore today Mrs. Shank called for me early. Her father and mother are going back in the machine, too. Phoned Jack to come for me.

Fallbrook. Hot weather!!! I did some shopping. Jack came for us about 4 p.m. and brought ice cream that we all ate before leaving. We came to Fallbrook, to hotel as Jack wants to see Mr. Westfall and go early to Bonsall.

June 4th - home to Palomar. Jack talked with Mr. Ben Thorpe who is with San Diego Farm Bureau, at Bonsall. He thinks favorably of the contract for Canfield orchards. At Pala, we left the machine and came on with the horse. Fearfully hot. I borrowed an umbrella for Catherine's sake. Papa took Catherine and me on from road camp at Uncle Nate's where we left Jack to work further.

It is very warm today. Stiff and tired from yesterday's long trip and holding Catherine.

Jack came home from roadwork. Mr. Westfall and three friends coming by stopped for supper. The Fishers came from Oceanside to camp near our house. They appointed Jack to oversee the road grade work.

Sunday—Jack spent most of the day at camp to look after belongings. I feel miserable still. County road supervisors investigating the hoped-for road are all here for dinner, nine men with chauffeurs. Papa took one pig down to sell, and we are glad we have not more than one left!

Wrote my "Palomar Paragraphs" for <u>Escondido Daily Times-Advocate</u>, June 18, 1919.

> Nellie—The Palomar grade is now in very good condition, repaired, and widened and ready for the automobiles, which have already begun to follow it to the beautiful mountaintop. Mecca of campers. The travelers add their appreciation to that of the mountain residents thanking our supervisor, Mr. Westfall, for his consideration. The boys worked hard and faithfully. Legislation is hoped for in one manner concerning the grade to prohibit the dragging of trees behind descending automobiles and wagons. Such extra brakes are not needed, and seriously injure the road.
>
> Dr. Milton Bailey came up the mountain again this last weekend. His friends were glad to have the opportunity to congratulate him on the arrival of the son, Gilbert Newton Bailey, who was born May 29. Mr. T.O. Bailey returned to San Diego with Dr. Bailey.
>
> P.B. Jolly of Valley Center was the guest of Harry Hill last Saturday.
>
> Cherries, now ripe on the mountain, have started to be gathered. It is a good year for them.
>
> Mrs. W. V. Fisher and daughter, Miss Frances Fisher of Oceanside, are camping at Nellie Post Office.

"Palomar Paragraphs" for <u>Escondido Daily Times-Advocate</u>, June 21, 1919:

W. V. Fisher and E. Fisher with Zona and William Fisher came from Oceanside Saturday to see Mrs. Fisher. The children, Zona and William will spend some time with their mother at her summer camp at Nellie Post Office.

A number of new campers are at the Palomar Hotel camping grounds this week. Some of them came up with Dr. Milton Bailey on Saturday. Mrs. Olive Griswold, of San Diego, arrived Wednesday for a visit of four or five days with her daughter, Mrs. Charles Mendenhall.

Sunday—Jack took all of us for a ride. He and I got fine wild strawberries near Boucher.

Jack went to Salmons' place for cherries to take to the Shanks. Mother helped me get ready to leave.

Elsinore—Jack and I left Catherine with mother and came down for me to see the doctor. Jack engaged a room for us at the Amsbury Hotel where we stayed the first night we were married. Elsinore is very hot. Dr. Shank thinks I will soon be in better health. We are sad over another loss of a baby. I miss my Catherine. Jack is lovely to me. I care for him beyond words.

Jack and I went to Perris where he arranged with Fred to buy a cow. We went to the movies.

This morning, after I had a final talk with the doctor, we left for Palomar and home.

Sunday—It is good to be home, especially with my dear baby again. Mrs. Fisher comes often, and she and her children joined us all in a Sunday sing and family prayers.

JULY

I feel that after this I surely will regain my usual health. I am weak but felt better this afternoon. Rested and read.

I finished writing my "Palomar Paragraphs" column for <u>Escondido Daily Times-Advocate</u>. Later my dear friend Fan Hand and I walked to

Chimney Flats. I feel much better. Jack came with the new cow, which dragged him and hurt his hand.

<u>Daily Times Advocate</u>, July 1, 1919:

> George Mendenhall, who returned from overseas about two weeks ago, was given his discharge from the service, visited the mountain on Tuesday.
>
> The Palomar Hotel has opened for the season. A camp fire Friday evening is to celebrate the glorious Fourth, and an out-of-door service is to be held Sunday afternoon.

I just read about the herd of thirteen elk the county supervisors have turned loose in the Mountains. The elk came from the Zoo in Balboa Park. They have passed a special ordinance protecting the herd.

Another forest fire has started on the south slope of Palomar but they expect to have it out in a couple days. We have had dry weather and east wind and with carelessness on the part of ranchers burning brush, we have such danger.

Independence Day—Alice and her family and Fanny and her man, Mr. Lance Estes, surprised us early in the morning. We had a big celebration dinner. We all went to a Fourth of July campfire near the hotel. Lance and Ernest sang. Ernest has such a rich voice and has been touring with an evangelist as his soloist, for some time.

Fan and her man keep going off on tramps, and this reminds Jack and me of our courting days in the Williams, Arizona, mountain country. I am wonderfully stronger.

Sunday—Jack took some of us to the Doane road and we walked down it to the Adams' place. All went in the afternoon to an open-air service conducted by Mr. Berger.

I baked. Jack and Aunt Mamie helped me wash. We women sat on the porch, sewed, talked, and looked after babies. We went to the Salmons' and picked cherries and a few black currants. Made jam, made out library report, cooked and cleaned. Jack moved Catherine's crib and my bed out-of-doors. I treasure sleeping outside. Fan and I walked to Faerie Wood near sunset.

Alice, Fan, and I walked to Doane Valley coming back by trail from Oliver place. I canned cherries and juice.

The mention of the Olivers in my journal brings back memories of their boys. The chief thing about Irwin and Ernest is that they were gentlemen. My sister, Alice knew the family better. In Long Beach, sometime around 1910, when she was a teenager, Irwin, though much older than she, was obviously much attracted to her, so we saw how ceremonious he was. Around that time, I was at our Palomar ranch with my parents when he was staying with us there. That meant rather primitive living conditions then, and our baths taken in the warm kitchen in a corrugated galvanized tub brought in for that purpose. And my chief memory of the Olivers is hearing Irwin saying very politely to my mother, "Mrs. Hayes I crave a bath." The Oliver orchard, still seen across the road from the state park residence between Silvercrest (now called State Park) and Doane Valley remains. When my husband Jack leased most of the apple orchards on the mountain, the Oliver orchard (then in good condition), was one of them. Josephine, Ernest's wife, told how she and Ernest used to hide notes in the crotch of a tree. Such a romantic memory.

Mid July I canned more cherries, made, and canned one quart of apricot marmalade. Sewed on the porch. Jack laid half of new floor in our kitchen. Every evening he and the Indian carpenter are working on Papa's log cabin, and now working on the sleeping porch. Papa took most of us to call on Mrs. Davis, whose log cabin is a marvel. Fan and I walked to the Point for larkspurs and sunset.

Fanny left early today. After our twenty years of friendship, it was very good to have her here.

Sunday—Jack took us to church in the auto and later to Boucher or nearest point by road. Aunt Mamie and I walked up with him from there, carrying Catherine. The folks all had dinner with us.

Yesterday I began making cherry jelly and canning and preserving cherries. It rained in the night, so we all who were sleeping out of doors moved our beds into the house. Cooked and helped clean house. I was expecting Salmons girls and Miss Berger for a Pomona College dinner. However, rain prevented Miss B. and the Salmons girls were soaked. I packed for our San Diego trip.

Jack, Catherine, and I left early for San Diego. Ate lunch at Oceanside, dinner at a good café in San Diego. We spent the night at the Broadway Hotel.

Traveled to Oceanside today. We shopped and Jack did many errands. He is seeing Mr. F. Salmons about pasture, employment agency for man, Fish Commissioner for fish, produce man about apples, etc. We plan to return to the mountain in two days.

We are home on Palomar—reached here about 2 o'clock. Good to be back though the trip was very pleasant. Found that the fox terrier we got from the pound in San Diego was gone already.

Sunday—We all had dinner as a house warming in the cabin. Alice and children are staying with us until they leave. Jack took Catherine and me to the Salmons to carry vegetables from San Diego to them. Alice and I walked to the out-of-doors service near the hotel. Sunday school classes

Log cabin built for Elsie's parents. Aunt Mamie in the middle, Farmerette on left.

continue outside. This was Mr. Berger's last service. Jack felt he had to take the horses and cows to new pasture.

Canned five quarts of cherries and cherry juice after picking, helped by Aunt Mamie, Junior and Dorothy. Also canned three quarts of tomatoes and one quart of string beans.

Jack helped me wash clothes especially by turning machine and wringer. Fred is unusually willing but does not know how to do some things.

Jack and I are looking after post office these days. Valenzuela, the Indian carpenter, left after finishing his work on cabin, porch and screen porch. We sent a telegram to Papa about a real estate letter. Hylinda telephoned for him to tell us that because of his lame back, they would not be back until later. I walked fast to Boucher's where Jack and Fred had already picked apples to take when Jack should go for them Saturday.

We took Catherine in her red cart to the woods, and Aunt Mamie and I picked wild gooseberries while Jack went farther to milk. Catherine crept far on the dusty road. Cleaned, cooked the gooseberries for jelly. Mr. Asher here for dinner. "Fearless entrepreneur" seems an apt summation for this mountain character. He is quite the artist. I have seen both paintings and photography that are his creations and they show such talent. Yet, he chooses to live alone, shifting between locations and endeavors to have as little baggage or ties as possible that would prevent his love of exploration. I think when he becomes too lonely he comes to us and pays or barters for meals with us.

Sunday—Went in Overland machine with Jack to the pasture near Silvercrest to milk.

Finished my wild gooseberry jelly, six glasses of it. Jack helped me wash clothes, and Aunt Mamie hung them, including extras such as blankets.

We had three rides in the Overland with Jack today. Twice he went to milk and once to the saddle, when he put up six signs along the grade, warning drivers not to drag trees. Mr. Asher stayed to lunch. Post office work and ironing.

Went in machine with Jack to call on Mrs. Hill, while he did errands. He looked at the nearby orchard, etc. George Mendenhall came to lunch and

Mr. Hill to supper (spur of the moment). We went to Boucher's with Jack and helped pick apples.

AUGUST

Jack left for Elsinore taking with him five boxes of apples. Mr. Asher here for supper.

Jack came home bringing Papa and Mama from Long Beach. Mr. Asher cut down some lilac today for Jack but thought it too hard work.

Sunday – We all went by team to Doane Valley. Jack caught seven brook trout. Cooked dinner on campfire and had restful time.

Jack saw three deer together at noon beside the orchard. Then saw one he thought was a different one and a wildcat all within an hour or so. Stanley Davis and George Mendenhall came to dinner by invitation. Jack and Fred mended fence.

We left to drive to San Diego today. After supper, we went as far as Oceanside. I miss Catherine already.

Reached San Diego early this morning, and I went with Jack to produce houses, etc. Bought a blouse, went to a play, "Baby Mine."

We went out in a launch to see the fleet come in. Very impressive. We went to another show after we saw friends.

Ready to start for home. Stayed over to bring hotel passengers. Went on board Navy destroyers, extremely interesting.

After four days away, we are home—Palomar. Mr. O'Toole and sons came with us from San Diego via Escondido. Good to be back, especially to see my baby.

Sunday—Jack took us to Silvercrest to deliver milk to the Smiths.

Jack and Fred worked on the grade, accomplishing much. Papa, Mother, Aunt Mamie, and I all picked early apples and crab apples. I climbed the trees. Catherine has taken a few steps alone and stands alone more and more.

Jack went to San Diego with good load of apples, crab apples and others. Aunt Mamie and I cut over ten trays of apples to dry.

Visiting the fleet in San Diego

Arranged our room and porch for Dr. Shank and family who are coming. Mopped floors, made pies. Jack came home bringing Rebecca S. and another passenger. At 9 p.m. Dr. and Mrs. Shank and boys appeared. The machine ran out of gas on the grade and left where it stopped. Jack and Dr. Shank went back for it.

Dr. Shank, Fred, and Jack hunted deer in vain. Mrs. Shank and I walked to lower Doane Valley and to French Valley Creek in afternoon. She played for Jack to sing Welsh songs in the evening.

Jack and Dr. Shank again hunted. Then we all went to Salmons' place. Birds had left only a few mulberries. There were no early pears. We went by machine and later to Boucher's, where we picked apples for the Shanks.

Sunday—Our guests are fine people we enjoy. Mrs. Shank and I rode horseback to the hotel. Jack, Catherine, and I had gone as far as Silvercrest where we were calling on campers when Dr. Shank ran back from below Doane Road to say his car was stuck in sand. Went back and pulled them out.

Jack left for San Diego with apples. Mr. Asher here for two meals, helping Papa and Fred pick Palomar Giants. Aunt Mamie and I cut apples to dry and I made thirteen glasses of jelly: mint, crab apple and chokecherry.

I finished nine more glasses of jelly and cut up apples. I helped with post office. Jack came up with three passengers. Then he went down the grade for more.

The campers that Jack helped up the grade late last night settled in Papa's tent house. We washed clothes and began drying more apples. Jack went down to get Hylinda and take mother to Long Beach. Rebecca Salmons went as far as Oceanside with them.

Post office work. Jack came with Hylinda—she is to help me with housework. Cooked the venison Mr. Elmore gave us. Went with Jack and Fred to the Adams place where we picked crab apples. With help, I canned what venison we had not eaten, two quarts.

Our campers take time. Finished some orange apple jelly and canned some apples. We have been drying them violently. Papa's cow has a new calf. I went with Jack to call at hotel. Then Jack took two passengers down to San Diego. Campers joined us in the house because of thunderstorm.

Post office and library work keep me busy when added to other duties. Papa left with the team for Escondido, taking apples for Jack who came back with passengers. Hylinda helped with big wash and ironed. I canned six quarts sliced apples. We sell small lots to campers and dry many besides those Jack takes down. I lost my wedding ring today while hanging laundry or perhaps while picking apples.

Jack left early with four passengers from hotel. He is a regular stage driver now. More post office work. Papa returned with a new man to work, Charles Stoesel. Hylinda baked bread – we had ten loaves. We went with Papa and camper children to Adams place to pick many Jonathans.

SEPTEMBER

The Longworths left, and the hotel really closed. Jack came back late from San Diego bringing Mrs. Bladen (now to live at hotel with her husband) and Mr. and Mrs. Young and a guest who were coming up in motorcycle with sidecar. I served them coffee. Hylinda helps a great deal.

I made peach preserves. Catherine walked about but seemed tired out by new use of muscles, cunning, staggering steps. Mr. Jolly was here for lunch. When we first knew our mail carrier, Mr. Jolly, he told us he had five little sons but was too shy to admit that his wife was pregnant. Mr. Jolly is a quiet little man who drives from his home in Valley Center on mail days to the foot of the mountain where his horse is waiting. Today was a stormy mail day and his shoes were soaking wet when he arrived. I suggested he come into the kitchen where the large woodstove sent out its warmth, take off his shoes and let them get as dry as possible. He put his cold feet in the oven while he ate his lunch. He was enjoying his coffee when called to the phone, located in the dining room. He came back, with a wide grin and announced, "I've got a girl."

Busy plum day. Canned twenty-three quarts and made five pints of the jam. I made a dozen glasses of plum jelly.

Sunday—Leisurely morning, though even Sundays are busy these days, cooking for so many. Mr. Steinbeck arrived to help with apples brought by his family, who called. Catherine is a dear with strangers about now.

Mrs. Galley called. Miss Smith called also. Charley left for Escondido. Mr. Asher began drying apples. Jack discharged Fred, who left.

Jack helped me change my canned fruit to the fine new cellar shelves. Still desperately busy with canning and now we are drying peaches too. Charlie hauled water for Hylinda to wash our clothes.

Began picking regular apples starting with Jonathans, on September 11. Mrs. Galley, Miss Smith, and Olga called on us. We cleaned house rather thoroughly, including pantry and post office lobby.

Dried sweet corn. Papa and Mother came back in the Overland, bringing Alice and her children and Uncle Ed. Little cousins are dear together. 100 boxes of Jonathans picked.

Cut peaches to dry and made sweet pickled peaches. Fruit this time comes from Boucher's orchard. Helped with post office. Jack left for San Diego about 6 a.m. Charley picked King apples.

Sunday—Jack got back from San Diego near noon. Catherine and her little cousins had a tea party.

Jack left for Elsinore and got back before supper bringing Martha Stanley to visit and help me with the housework.

Poor traveler Jack left again, this time for San Diego once more. Martha and Hylinda both worked with me.

Jack brought Grace, Mrs. Steinbeck and a packer, Mr. Swain, up from San Diego. There is so much work with the apples and cooking for the hired help.

Hylinda and Uncle Ed went down the mountain with Jack when he left for San Diego today. Hylinda thought she ought to go as Martha is going to help me and Grace wants to stay as farmerette. She worked as picker half-day. The Steinbecks board here still though staying at Silvercrest.

The Steinbecks here for lunch as well as other boarders. Pears canned, preserves made, etc. Takes ever so long to prepare them.

Sunday—Aunt Mamie went for a picnic with Mother, Papa, Alice, and children. Grace, Martha, and I walked to upper Doane while Jack and Cati stayed home. The men, Smiths, and our people came to sing hymns.

Miss Smith and Olga called. Fine weather. Martha and I made cider and apple butter and took pictures.

Martha and I had a washday by the ram. Work began on Cleaver Orchard, and she and I took the lunch over there and shared it with the others, a good time.

Work on Cleaver Orchard is finished. Truck came up and took down 125 packed boxes. Papa and Mother see to the mail these days. George Mendenhall and his bride stopped for a few minutes. Mr. Allen K. Wright of Long Beach, a writer, came up to pick apples. Picking on our place now.

A few light showers, but Jack left for San Diego to see about getting more paper wraps and boxes. I rested in the afternoon and read The Man Thou Gavest Me by Harriet Comstock. It is good.

Rain and fog in earnest so the work on the apples cannot go on. Martha and I try to cheer the men with good meals. Girls canned pears for themselves. Jack got back late from San Diego.

Sunday—Ever so wet outside. Mr. Wright in the evening gave us readings of some of his poems, and we sang hymns, men too.

Left—Hylinda and Alice on horseback; Right—Elsie hiking in her fabulous boots.

Rain, mist and fog still. We girls, with Mother's help, tied a comfort of mine. I made bread. Weather cleared after 1 ¾ inches of rain in the storm, so we girls walked.

OCTOBER

Jack got back from San Diego with an elderly gentleman (really) to pick apples. Mr. Quarles, an interesting type. Truck stuck on grade. Mr. Gorton, Horticultural Commissioner, and man with him and Mr. Webb had a late afternoon lunch here.

Jack had the five men all work on the grade, and great improvements made on it after the recent injuries of wet weather.

Canned grape juice. Aunt Mamie helps a great deal with Catherine. Mother had interesting news from Hylinda. I went with Jack in machine to Cleaver orchard. Jack went down the grade and brought my cousin Sadie back.

Sadie's first day of farmeretting for this year. We washed clothes.

Jack went to Oceanside, taking twelve boxes of apples to Wisdoms and came back in afternoon. Mr. Quarles left, as work picking scattering apples, high in trees at Boucher's orchard was too hard for him. We took lunch to Mr. Swain and Sadie who worked at Silvercrest.

Truck came with Mr. Shook for 500 boxes. Mr. And Mr. Salmons and Elizabeth Bailey called. Martha and I walked over to Silvercrest taking hot soup and fresh cake to add to the men's and Sadie's lunch. I counted my canned fruit by list. Have put up over 300 jars since June.

Last apples at Boucher's picked today. They are packed at Silvercrest. Charlie killed a calf. Several sets of people came for apples, culls, in answer to Jack's advertisements. Three extra here for dinner.

Sunday—We had Mr. Webb and some friends to dinner, thirteen again, same as last night. Jack went to San Diego in afternoon. The Grahams and Bohannans from Elsinore came up and took down apples and cider.

Very busy day. We washed and I canned seven quarts of calf and one of beef. Martha picked apples for two hours. Jack came back with two new pickers, younger men (for Martha and Sadie)!

Mr. Webb brought truck again and had lunch as usual. He brought me four boxes of fine Muscat grapes. Canned fifteen quarts of them and gave mother one box. I finished some quince jelly. Catherine ran away with Dorothy and Jr. to the ram. Work at Silvercrest is finished.

Last of the apples on this place are being picked. Some of the men picked in Doane Valley. Jack went to Oceanside, reaching home in early evening with supplies as usual. He is a splendid provider! We girls planned a feast for tomorrow and wrote limericks for it.

Picking on Adams place began. Martha and I were very busy with the seven-course birthday dinner, a stag affair for the men. Place cards by Alice, etc. They were surprised and pleased. Lots of fun.

Sunday—Jack has insisted that we girls have a holiday, and he would see to men's lunch. So we left table set, pies made, beans cooking, and went with girls and all of the relatives except Jack beyond Sunday School Flats. Some of us went to Davis' cabin. The Danes, Roots and Wares were here when we got home. Men came to sing hymns.

Truck came up. Three men with truck extra for lunch today. Packing was begun today in Adams' orchard. Catherine played happily in orchard with her cousins.

Apple wagon with Catherine following after Jack.

Jack took Catherine and me in the machine with lunch to Adams' orchard. Sadie and I helped sort apples. We got back in time to start dinner. Storm seems to be coming.

Last night and today over 2 ½ inches of rain fell. We wish we might have had even two more days of good weather, but are glad storms have not bothered more. Six men still here, Messrs. Swain, Loftus, Matthews, Stoesel, Edman and Ray.

On Halloween, we had a special dinner for the men.

―――――

Again this year, the intensity of apple season work took me away from my journaling. To give an idea of what that work entailed, here are some notes I recorded at the time:

By Oct. 21, I had done 68 pints jam, 13 glasses preserves, 94 glasses jelly, 11 pints sweet pickle, 17 quarts fruit juice, 12 bottles fruit juice, 105 quarts canned fruit, 10 quarts meat, 4 quarts vegetables.

Apples Sold 1919:

> August 23 – 111 boxes of Jonathans
> October 7 – 96 boxes Golden
> October 17 – 98 boxes Spits Newtons
> October 22 – 170 boxes Newtons
> October 22 – 93 boxes unknown
> Total shipped 560 boxes apples
> Cold storage on 481 boxes at $0.28 came to $134.68

7

Travelers at Our Door
1920

Who Has Seen the Fairies?
By Elsie R. H. Roberts

It's harder to find fairies
If you live in a city—
But if you never see one,
Oh, that is a pity!

Country children spy them,
Flitting through a wood,
Dancing in a meadow—
Sometimes, if they're good!

But even if you live
On a busy, crowded street,
And think there's not a single spot
For fairy folk to meet,

Watch! One may come frolicking
From a far-off hill,
Sliding down a sunbeam
To your windowsill.

Little Catherine thrived on the clean mountain air, apples and dirt. We purchased a wooden pen for her protection. It looked like a little miniature horse corral, and it kept her in the dirt, but safe. Palomar was such a glorious setting in which to raise a family

When we first made our move to the mountain, we had no idea that it would become more than our own private home. We were in a most wonderful location, on the crest of Palomar Mountain. Beauty lovers were always climbing the long grade to camp in the forest or stay at our neighbors' summer resort.

We had plenty of guests ourselves as all our relatives and friends came to the ranch to visit us. Though the Bailey mountain resort closed in winter, many venturesome travelers came up to see the snow; and sometimes they knocked at our door and begged us to serve them a meal. In the wilds, one cannot turn people away hungry.

One winter day came when our supplies happened to be a little low (that does happen sometimes thirty miles from town), an automobile arrived full of starving strangers.

"Just give us anything!" they implored. "We don't care what we get or what we pay, just so we're fed."

We shrugged our shoulders and did our best, but we said to each other that night, "If we had a real hotel we'd always have supplies."

Once when we had entertained several groups in immediate succession, we looked at each other in agreement. "We're almost in the hotel business right now."

Then one day we had a call from Milton Bailey who owned the summer resort nearby. "Just up for the weekend." he said. "Not going to open this year." Milton had married lovely Adalind sometime earlier, but when they were up in the summers, we did not see much of them in such busy times.

So, when we understood that Milton Bailey was not reopening his resort (though he did, after all), we started a much smaller one of our own. We called it Planwydd—Jack's middle name. In Welsh, it means planted tree, pronounced "planwyth."

We laughed once we considered and imagined the summer hordes coming down upon us, all dressed up in their outing togs and no place to go! Our guests were largely lawyers, bankers, or doctors.

And we were much amused when people cried, "How did you ever decide so suddenly to do such a thing?"

One dark night a month or so later, we were at dinner when we heard a car, and then a knock. A man entered with his hat in his hand. He bowed low, and announced dramatically,

"We crave your mercy! We thought the hotel was open. The two ladies of our party are exhausted, and feel that they simply cannot go down that terrible grade tonight. There are five of us. Could you . . . won't you . . . in Christian charity put us up for the night?"

We looked about at the relatives and friends then visiting us. We counted beds.

"We fellows will sleep outdoors if only our wives can have a room," suggested the man, not abating his role of a supplicant.

And so it we arranged things. But, oh, how the wind blew that night! "If we only call this a hotel, we'd see to it that we had more room for travelers," we remarked aside.

During the spring, the neighbors and added workers from below made our house their headquarters while they mended the roads. It really was in the most convenient place. As we knew they were to be there, we acquired more dishes and more tents as sleeping quarters. We often had a large bonfire. We would roast ears of corn and potatoes. The cook would bring a great covered pan of fried chicken from the house. Soon afterward, we opened our mountain hotel.

FROM MY JOURNAL JANUARY, 1920

New Year's Day—Palomar Mountain. No special New Year celebration.

Charlie with us but Ray not back yet. Mrs. Hill called. I always laugh when I think of Alice Hill. Sometimes we made mountain friends because of necessity and sometimes because they were unique and fascinating individuals. Alice had toured with movie magnate Cecil DeMille. The story

Left—Palomar soon became an attraction for motorists; Right—Catherine loved climbing apple trees

circulated that fifty dollars given her to buy a wedding gown she spent instead on a riding habit, tailor-made for her of a very beautiful material. Rather than washing her clothes, she would hang them on the clothesline for three weeks to air.

Jack and Charlie went to Mendenhall's to use dynamite on some trees. Rained, so I invited Mr. Jolly in for hot lunch. Heard of Hylinda's engagement to Absalom Urshan and are much excited. They hope to marry soon. Hylinda is thirty-five years old, and I have heard that Absalom is forty. Hylinda wrote explaining that his first wife and children had been killed in in the 1915 Assyrian genocide in Persia. Only his eleven-year-old son, Sargis, survived.

Sunday—Catherine more interesting all the time, she talks a great deal.

Belated announcement arrived that had gone astray of marriage of Hylinda and Absalom Urshan! We are terribly excited and very glad for her. Mother and Alice wrote well of him.

Jack, Ray and Charles are gone to work on the grade. I cooked extra food repeatedly for workers camping down grade for roadwork.

Yesterday, January 10, a very cold day, Robert Asher came by the post office with a package of sixteen skins he wants shipped to Funston Bros. in Missouri. He told us it is one coyote, three fox, three lynx cat, one badger, three coons and five skunks. Robert is quite the trapper and he knows how to tell a great story.

Today, Mr. Asher showed up at our house with a badly injured hand. Jack and I quickly got his hand into an almost boiling hot solution of potassium permanganate. Inspection of his hand after removal of blood revealed two fingers gnashed—but no bones touched. Mr. Asher told us the story while we worked on his injury. He had been out working his trap lines. One of the coyotes had pulled the light drag into a big ceanothus [lilac] bush and had tangled himself up.

Mr. Asher did not have a gun with him, there was no room to swing a club, and the coyote was too much alive to allow him to untangle his chain. He said he figured on the proposition for a while. He had a three-foot long leather strap along. Thinking that if he could only get the strap over the coyote's head and under his neck he would have him about where he wanted him. At least that is what he figured on. He fastened one end of the strap to a long stick, arranged a loop on the other end of strap, slipped the loop over the animal's head and partway under his chin, and there it stuck. Coyote began snapping at the strap—if he once caught it, good-bye strap!

Mr. Asher said there was no time for halfway measures. He eased himself into the bush, reached gingerly for the strap and worked it under the canine's throat. That is what he thought he was doing, but he actually had his hand well back in the creature's mouth. Mr. Coyote knew what to do and he did it. Mr. Asher managed to jerk his hand out covered with blood and ruined entirely, at least it seemed that way.

He promptly abandoned the coyote to his fate and knowing our home was near he headed for us. While we were working with his hand, Charlie Stoessel went over and shot the coyote. Mr. Asher certainly knows how to tell a story!

Jack bought $42 worth of groceries from the Bladens who are going down on account of Mrs. B's rheumatism. As mountain folk living far from supplies and dependent on each other, we sometimes barter back and forth.

Sunday—Mr. and Mrs. Bladen stopped to say good-bye on their way down. We are sorry to see them go. Mr. and Mrs. Mendenhall and Mrs. Salmons called. Mrs. Salmons much interested in Hylinda's marriage and the pictures of Hylinda and Absalom we received.

Kenneth Beach had lunch with us. Milton stopped with meat and shoes for Catherine he brought from San Diego for us. He came to bring Mr. and Mrs. Smith to stay at hotel. Jack went to San Diego with Milton to see about naturalization papers. Warm weather compared to just a few days ago. Mrs. Hill called. I repeatedly walked to the Hills to give the phone messages or to call. Nice letter from Absalom.

January 20—Aunt Mamie is seventy-four today. Miss Thalia Hatheway (of San Diego), census enumerator, came to stay a week with us while taking the mountain census. Mrs. Davis, Mrs. Salmons and Kenneth Beach called.

We took lunch to the Cleaver orchard where Jack was pruning. Pleasant time.

Aunt Mamie, Catherine, and I went to the Cleaver orchard again, taking lunch for the three men now pruning and dragging brush there. Called on Mrs. Hill.

FEBRUARY

Mr. Salmons and Kenneth stayed for lunch when they came for mail. Charlie went to meet Webb Brothers at Tin Can Flats for cider barrels.

Sunday—The Danes and Shanks surprised us in the rain, and stayed all night.

Raining hard all day but Shanks and Danes left after early lunch.

We had four and one-half inches of snow on February 10. Mr. Asher, Mr. Mendenhall and Mr. Jolly had lunch with us.

Jack and Charlie working on the grade below the snow line. Sunshine.

Sunday—Went to the Point. Signs of spring! Mr. Asher began boarding with us; he will pay with fox skins for furs for us.

Jack took Papa and Mama down to foot of grade in machine and he walked back in heavy rain.

Rained again last night, windy and still raining today. Robert Asher is here. He skinned one fox, a coon and a bobcat. Jack skinned one fox for him.

Mr. Jolly late due to high river, he came in to lunch, as did Kenneth.

Sunday—Washington's Birthday. We played phonograph and showed patriotic pictures to hired men to celebrate. Rain still. Seven baby chicks hatched much to Catherine's delight. Catherine calls the baby chicks "my peeps." Robert Asher settled his bill with us. He credited Jack with one dollar for skinning two fox for him. His board was from Feb. 17 to Feb 25 - 8 1/3 days at $1.10 per day.

MARCH

Mr. Asher is still with us, but the trapping season has closed now that March has begun. He is hunting for snails now. A shell collector, Mr. Lowe of Long Beach, buys them from him. He is also pruning apple trees for us on the Adams' place.

One of the cows got loose and Mrs. Hill and I trailed it to the Pedley place. Then I walked to Adams' place to tell Jack and drove back with him. Ray and Mr. Asher are helping prune there. I repeatedly walked to the Hills to give the phone messages or to make a call.

March 5—Aunt Annie's birthday. Aunt Mamie told me much about her while we sewed. The men finished plowing part of Boucher's. We have only our usual boarders again now, since Mr. Asher left for El Cajon.

Sunday—Beautiful day and a delightful drive. Jack took Aunt Mamie, Catherine, and me to Boucher's. We carried our lunch. Walked down the mountainside where two deer ran below us. Yellow violets and peas in bloom.

The boys went to Boucher's with camping outfit to stay three days or so. They are plowing the orchard. I cooked extra food for them to take.

By now, they should be almost through with the plowing. Took food to last some time, camping there last night, but driven home by storm tonight.

Mrs. Bailey, children, and Mrs. Sadler are at the hotel for a while and are to get milk from us. I am making summer housedresses for Catherine and me. Catherine's birthday present from the Welsh grandparents came early, a dear little gold ring that fits well.

I am busy getting things cooked for the boys to take doughnuts, pies, bread, and cake. Mail days are always busy and swift. Mrs. Sadler called.

Sunday—Aunt Mamie, Catherine, and I went to Ray's place with Jack and the boys, taking them and their things over, as they are to prune their buttercups out. Fog hurried us home.

Jack is now plowing the Cleaver Orchard. We took his lunch over, enjoying a pleasant walk and picnic. I worked on carpet rags.

Mr. Jolly and George Mendenhall and his wife had a half-meal here, not a square one this time. Stormy weather.

We awoke to a beautiful world of snow. I walked over it to give Mrs. Hill a phone message. Fog really added to the beauty, but then sun melted it all fast. Catherine trots about the yard after her daddy with great joy, interested in everything. Winter does not make an indoors child of her. The eight cats let her do anything with them. She carries them about by the neck or picks them up by the tail. Aunt Mamie frequently serves as baby sitter for Catherine. One day she changed her clothes five times.

Perfect day. Finished orange and grapefruit peel.

Sunday—Stormy day, so we all stayed in the house. We even ate in the living room. Boys were supposed to come today, but of course did not in this weather.

One baby chick hatched yesterday. Rain, hail and snow. Did some extra mending and worked on carpet rags. Nice family day.

Mr. Jolly did not come, the first time he has ever missed bringing the mail. Much snow, Ray and Charlie came back anyway.

Great fun taking Catherine out on her little red sled which Jack nailed a box on for her. Now over ten inches of snow in this storm, with fog and rain today. Took an extra rest and finished reading <u>The Lighted Match</u>, pleasant tale.

Mr. Jolly came, the first time this week. He had four horses pull his Ford across the river though.

Sunshine this morning. We put Catherine on her sled again and took four more pictures of her in the snow. Fog came later. Mr. Jolly came for his usual Saturday mail delivery.

Ray got a fish bone (smoked herring) in his throat and left to see a doctor! Jack and the boys began painting woodwork and ceilings.

APRIL

Catherine has bunnies sent her. We celebrated C's birthday with cake and two candles. She is a darling two years old. We often place Catherine in a box under the apple tree while Aunt Mamie and I hoe up morning glory pests. Ray came back from San Diego, his father coming too. That makes three hired men at a time now, pruning and plowing in various orchards.

 Sunday- Easter and a beautiful day, Catherine and I went through snow patches to Chimney Flats, but did not find violets. Called on Mrs. Hill in the afternoon and got a pruning saw there for Jack.

Carl Mendenhall came from down below with a man interested in the timber. I made our library circulation report. Indians brought my trunk from Pala, sent there from Elsinore. What fun unpacking things I had not seen for two years!

Early this morning I went to the Adams' place. Jack started the Indians plowing and the boys finished pruning there today.

Two days later the men are planting plum and pear trees, but had to stop in the afternoon because of heavy fog that later turned to rain. Basted hems in three new sheets and washed pillow ticking.

Sunday—Baked bread and made two loaves buttermilk nut bread, nine loaves in all. Post office work on this beautiful spring morning. Went to Inspiration Point and found yellow peas and buttercups. We made orange ice using snow from left over patch for freezing.

Foggy and cold, but Jack walked part way down grade to look after roadwork. Catherine helped me plant peas. We gave Mr. Jolly cocoa and soup. Rain. Finished the two bed pillows I made from an old bolster. Catherine asks Mr. Jolly first thing, "Bring Catrin package?"

Blizzard on April 16th! Helen was supposed to come this weekend. She phoned, and I had to tell her she could not make the grade. Jack fears harm from storm to fruit. Worked on a dress for Catherine out of scraps of blue linen left from a dress I had new when engaged!

We have fog and light rain again. The road near our house put into splendid condition now.

Planted more vegetable seeds. Went to Chimney Flats for our lunch and gathered violets. Cleaned cellar.

MAY

The violets are beautiful at Chimney Flats.

———

Again this year the hotel work, boarders, and apple season drew me away from my journal. I just seem to have too much to do. When we decided to turn the apple ranch into a resort, we built six rustic one-room bedroom guest cabins scattered over the property. We also had a number of tents for the same purpose. The many guests, mostly professional people coming up from the cities, greatly added to my work. I only kept brief notes after this.

———

June 4—Served dinner to four people, three dollars.

June 20—Fan and Lance came for a two weeks honeymoon in the log cabin. While Papa and Mama moved in with us for that time.

July 3—Seven guests for supper and the night. One lady occupied our bedroom—one dollar.

July 9—Alonzo, Sadie and I went to the Frazier place. I took over fifty pounds of honey from a hive. We spent the next day straining honey—three gallons.

Lovely to have this nice article in the "Times" telling about Jack and our apples.

Harvesting Apple Crop

Escondido *Daily Times Advocate*, September 24, 1920

PALOMAR FRUIT TO BE HAULED BY AUTO TRUCKS TO SAN DIEGO—BETTER ROADS NEEDED

Jack P. Roberts, of Palomar Mountain, was in Escondido Tuesday rustling pickers and packers for the harvest of his crop of apples on the big hill, where, within the next three weeks, he will corral the product of more than 100 acres of choice orchard, either leased or controlled by him.

"I have no need to tell you," says Roberts, "that apples grow to perfection on Palomar. I agree with the recently adopted slogan: 'There'll be nothing to mar Palomar,' as soon as we get the roads fixed up. It's a cinch that more persons have been on Palomar this summer than for many years."

"Speaking again of apples, diseases peculiar to them are practically unknown. Our annual rainfall which last winter was better than 50 inches, or more than five times greater than the precipitation at San Diego city, or the coast, makes irrigation unnecessary. Early varieties of apples do as well as the late ones. All of the popular varieties do well. The Palomar Giants and the Arkansas Beauties, which grow on the mountain, deserve to be better known. In my opinion the latter excel the far-famed Jonathan in size, flavor and keeping qualities; while the Giants are worthy of their name, weighing sometimes more than a pound."

A. G. Hayes, father-in-law of Roberts, owns one of the attractive apple ranches on the mountain. It is at Nellie – the name by which the mountain post office is known but which may be changed to Palomar in the near future, as soon as a few yards of red tape can be unwound. Roberts has under lease the orchards owned by the C. A. Canfield estate. He is a strong advocate of the Whitney method of pruning, which he employed last season.

On September 3, 1920—Jack became an American citizen by naturalization and Catherine and I became Americans through him. However, I was always an American until I married Jack!

8

From Alien to Postmistress
1921-1923

Madame Lofty
By Elsie R. H. Roberts

Mrs. Lofty has a carriage,
So have I.
She has dappled grays to draw it,
So have I.
She's no fonder of her coachman,
Than am I.
With my blue-eyed laughing baby
Tumbling by,
I hide his face, least she should see
My cherub boy and envy me.

Her fine husband has white fringes,
Mine has not,
He can give his bride a palace,
Mine a cot,
Hers comes home beneath the starlight
Never cares she,
Mine comes in the purple twilight,
Kisses me,
And prays that he who holds life's sands
May hold his loved ones in his hands.

Mrs. Lofty has her jewels
So have I,
She wears hers upon her bosom
Inside I,
She will bear the treasure with me,
When I die,
For I have love, and she has gold,
She counts her wealth,
Mine can't be told.

She has those who love her station,
Some have I,
But I've one true heart beside me,
Glad am I
I'd not change it for a kingdom
No, not I
God will weigh it in the balance,
By and by
And then the difference He'll define
'Twixt Mrs. Lofty's wealth and mine.

For people living on a remote mountain where neighbors were scattered, winter afforded idle hours and allowed times to read, write, and take vigorous tramps through the snow. Mountain residents often made their visits in the winter by horseback, sometimes in deep snow. Jack's work had been hard, and he had been troubled repeatedly by an ulcer. Relaxing seldom occurred during the fall and summer season. Guests and apple picking consumed our time. He welcomed the less busy season of the winter months and spent much time reading.

ENTRIES FROM MY JOURNAL, 1921

JANUARY

New Year's Day—Palomar Mountain. Now that Jack has become a citizen they no longer consider me as an alien. I applied for the position of Postmaster. While the men hunted, we walked on the hills. Gratitude and resolutions.

Jack made Catherine a wheelbarrow just her size. She played out all day. Billy, the horse, is sick.

Billy became worse during the night and Jack worked with him from 3 a.m. on and most of the day today. We are canning chickens to save feed and have jars ready to open. Now we have finished the first set of chickens with six birds making eight quarts, filling boiler for cold pack process. We are eating giblets stew and necks!

After three days of sickness, the poor horse died last night despite Jack's care. So Jack left by auto to look for another. Olin is cremating. Cleaned six more roosters.

Sunday—Very happy day. Catherine rode in front of me in saddle on Boy (horse) while Jack walked with gun to Mendenhalls. Heard a mountain lion. George and Agnes came back with us calling enroute on Davises for dinner and the evening.

On January 10, we woke to find snow. Catherine loves playing out in it in her rubber boots we gave her for Christmas. We finished canning roosters, fourteen altogether within a week, with a total of nineteen quarts.

Today it is clear. This storm brought over three inches of snow. George Mendenhall and Marion Davis with her baby and Bob stayed after mail for lunch. Washday, hanging clothes in sunshine over the snow. Jack hunted, getting birds for Mr. Jolly.

Made butter, sending a pound to Aunt Mamie for her birthday. There are always tasks to be done. Jack is now very busy pruning blackberry and raspberry vines.

Sunday—Catherine and I walked to Silvercrest and enjoyed it ever so much. Patches of snow covered about half the way. Catherine is growing up surrounded by nature's classroom, and I delight in teaching her about my mountain. Life is full and fulfilling. Two paying guests for dinner. Several autos came up the grade. It looks like we are in for a storm again.

This morning we awoke to rain, snow, sleet, also wind. Mr. Jolly came in for lunch, with cocoa as usual for him in bad weather. Catherine revels in her toy cupboard when she needs to stay indoors.

Another day and snow still coming. Making small aprons for myself and for Catherine, also doll clothes for her to reward her for learning to take her nap alone in afternoons.

Catherine goes out to play once or twice a day during this lasting storm, whether snow is falling or not. She loves it. Jack's stomach is bothering him again. He is trying an extremely strict diet of toast, eggs and purees. I baked bread and made butter.

Sunday—After six days of stormy weather, it cleared in the afternoon, and I took snow pictures. Catherine plays hours alone most happily, really not quite alone, as she's always going after the dogs and cats. Mr. W. Beach here for overnight.

This week we have had a few hours of decent weather. Jack has pruned about sixty trees when it is not too stormy.

By today, we have lovely sunshine so Jack went down to look at the grade again. He often meets my parents or others on the grade to help bring up a load or to drive the machine the rest of the way. Mr. Salmons stayed for lunch. His wife is still with her mother, Mrs. Bailey, who is very ill in San Diego. I got some apples ready to mail.

End of the month and it is rainy again. Mr. Oliver and a friend came up in a Dodge and had dinner with us. I wrote on a story in the afternoon and evening.

FEBRUARY

We began the month in Escondido. Jack, Catherine, and I left after mail time and came here. We had dinner and a delightful time with Mr. and Mrs. Rose who have leased the Charlotta Hotel.

On to San Diego today—Hotel Tioga. Reached San Diego about noon after Jack bought a wagon and disc at Escondido. Doctor Jessop tested my eyes. I took Catherine to see the animals at Balboa Park, later we went to a show.

We left San Diego this morning around 11 a.m. and lunched at Capistrano. Spending the day in Alhambra, surprising the family at suppertime. Jack went on to Wilmington to buy a tank. Lovely to be here and all seem well. Alice's third child, Beatrice Elsie, has surely grown. Papa took us in his auto to call on Hylinda. Her baby Sarah is darling, very gentle. Jack came for Catherine and me, and we called on the family again.

Heading back, we are stopping tonight at the Amsbury Hotel in Elsinore. Such sweet memories this hotel has for us.

After five days away, we are back on Palomar Mountain. We brought our new dog. He seems particularly good. The drive up the grade was in fog and rain, arriving just as Mr. Jolly came.

Sunday—Snowing today

Terrifying experience today, Catherine was lost near twilight. It was a nightmare of terror. Men checked for tracks in the snow and thought she was not gone, but I had called and hunted all over the house. Crazed with fear of a mountain lion I ran the way she had once started to toddle towards Silvercrest, calling her name. I knew she could not have gone so far, and I could run no more. Thankfully, she had dropped to sleep out of sight inside the house and we found her behind a dresser placed at an angle from the wall. Oh, so grateful to find her here!

Jack went down the grade with Mr. Hill to bring back our new wagon and disc. He came back with four men, one of whom left after lunch. Mr. Wright, Mr. Fisher, and Mr. Casson are to stay to work for us.

Jack took the horses to Barker Canyon with the men, all gone, all day. Glorious weather, Catherine and I went on a picnic below the Point and brought back ferns. We did a big baking and made puff pastry for lemon cheese. I picked pussy willows.

We looked in vain for Adelphi people that Jack expected, but an auto load of Oceanside people came. Jack, Catherine, and I walked to Doane Valley for the horses and came back part of the way bareback.

Mid-month and it snowed nearly all day. We are experiencing winter suddenly again after summer weather. Now about 3 ½ inches snow. Made four pounds of butter. The sun on snow is glorious, white, silver with vivid blue of sky, and green of evergreens. We had a delightful sleigh ride to Silvercrest and in the afternoon, we called on the Hills and the Davises.

Winter, with fewer guests and less apple work, allows time to visit neighbors. Yesterday we went horseback to the Salmons, Catherine in front of me on Sadie and Jack on Boy. Bought a new horse there and had dinner and a lovely time. Baby blue eyes and filaree in bloom. Today a blizzard brought Jack home in a hurry after he went to help Stanley cut wood. New man, Mr. Snow, came to work. Heard Primary Plans accepted my "Valentines."

I include this news article to show how devastating winter weather can be when you have an apple ranch. We enjoy the snow but our hearts sorrow when it destroys the apple blossoms.

Escondido Daily Times Advocate February 19, 1921
Heavy Fog Kills Palomar Fruit

Trees covered with congealed moisture, which falls to ground at sunrise.

Planwydd

This morning before Old Sol put Jack Frost to flight this grand old mountain was gorgeous with a heavy coating of congealed moisture formed by the fog which swept in from the coast yesterday running into a temperature of twenty degrees above zero.

Jack Roberts at Planwydd said Jack Frost had a bigger hand last night than ever before. The chances being that all of the deciduous fruit was destroyed. Practically all of the apple, peach and prune trees were in full blossom. The fog enveloped every blossom in a thick coating of ice, causing them to resemble flowers under ice.

The saw is at our place now and a huge pile of cut wood rejoices our hearts. The Davis and Mendenhall families were here for dinner, the men helping cut wood and the girls helping with the dinner. Pleasant time. Jack drove Mother and Papa to the foot of the grade in machine and he walked back.

Fog came up and turned into rain. I did a large part of the washing in the kitchen and baked rolls, bread, and biscuits. Today I revised the story written largely a week ago. More wood cut.

Jack left for San Diego taking Mr. Snow, who does not know how to work on a ranch. Mr. McClard went with Stanley to Mesa Grande for oats. I am doing a lot of typing on stories and revel in it. Catherine and I walked below the orchard and found many baby blue eyes.

After two days away, Jack got back from San Diego with a new man today. He is Gus Weber, a Swiss, who seems to understand ranch work. Olin and Mr. McClard to work on the road again.

Sunday—At 1:40 a.m., Mr. & Mrs. Taylor came up! The men came to see the timber. Jack went with them to Mendenhalls.

MARCH

I began the month doing a great deal of typing on a story, revising it. I surely enjoy this sort of thing. We sent off post office reports for

Left—Elsie takes over as postmistress.
Right—Catherine in front of Nellie Post
Office at Planwydd

February. While Gus was making a garden or getting the ground ready for it, Jack, Catherine, and I drove to Mendenhall Valley and had dinner with Agnes and George. Lovely day.

Gus is plowing the Oliver place. In the afternoon, Jack and I went to Boucher's orchard to prune fruit trees. Catherine and I went by horseback to join him. Pear, plum, and peach blossoms! Jack helped me churn afterwards. Elated to receive notice of my appointment as Postmaster at Palomar Mountain. I already had been doing most of the work as deputy. Hylinda and family, except Absalom (Sarah and Sargis) had a long stay with the folks at the cabin here.

Jack burned off grass at Chimney Flats. The weather looks uncertain and is foggy. I sent off one story for publication and some verses.

Jack and Gus have been using grader. Found a yellow violet. Weather prevented us going to Barker Canyon with the Mendenhalls as planned. We walked to Silvercrest.

After mid-March, our hotel boarders came so steadily that I was more than busy, and I did not keep much of a diary for the rest of year.

WHO does not feel the lure of the mountain trail that winds through great forests and along the edge of the world? In vacation-time the cool green woods call one to their beauty and peace and silence. Come to Palomar Mountain and look down from the forests of oak and fir to the ocean beyond the lower ranges.

Visit San Louis Rey and Pala Missions en route, spend Sunday on Palomar, and cross over the mountain, going down to Warner's.

Spend your vacation at "PLANWYDD"

Home-cooked meals. Saddle horses. Trips arranged.

One can explore a new peak or canyon every day for a month. A profusion of ferns and wild flowers. Look from Los Angeles to Mexico.

"Nothing to mar beautiful Palomar"

RATES AT "PLANWYDD"

Board and Room (single) by the day	-	-	$3.25
" " " " " " week	-	-	20.00
" " " (double) " " day	-	-	3.00
" " " " " " week	-	-	18.50

Cabins and tents. Housekeeping accommodations if desired.

Telephone Palomar Mountain, through Pala, and make arrangements to go up in one of our machines, or call Main 7020 Tioga Hotel, San Diego.

Planwydd Resort brochure

The Harnett family of Long Beach

We made a trip to Long Beach, visiting family, the Harnetts, and other friends. Aunt Mamie was wintering with my parents. She came back to the mountain with us April 1.

By April 18, Papa and Mama were back on the mountain but Papa had such a terrible cold that they left the mountain again May 31 and went to Alice's home in Alhambra. The folks came back and forth to the mountain after that.

I am thrilled when I see newspaper articles referring to our place here.

SEEK GOOD ROADS UP MOUNTAIN

San Diego's Back Country Playgrounds to be Boosted at Planwydd Celebration

From *L.A. Times* May 1, 1921

PALOMAR MOUNTAIN, April 30

The good roads, barbecue, bonfire and other attractions of the celebration to be staged at Planwydd, Saturday, May 7, will bring motorists from many sections of the Southland, and it is expected that the gathering will result in much constructive work along the lines of the betterment of the mountain roads of the backcountry of San Diego County.

Arrangements have been made by the Supervisors of San Diego County for the construction of a good road up the east side of the mountains, the slowness of the development of grazing purposes having been due to lack of road facilities.

The barbecue will be served in Chimney Flat, Planwydd Camp, at 4 p.m., and will be followed by drives to the various points of interest, the bonfire being kindled on Inspiration Heights at 8:30 o'clock.

Louis S. Salmons is president of the Palomar Mountain Good Roads Association, Jack P. Roberts, vice-president, George Mendenhall, treasurer, who with Dr. Milton Bailey, William Beach, and E. R. McClard, composes the board of directors. J.H. Heath, secretary of the Escondido Chamber of Commerce, is the secretary, Escondido being the headquarters of the organization.

August 11—Sadie, Hylinda and I went to the Frazier Place. Alice and I took over the job of straining over three gallons of honey

August 22, Sunday—Served twenty-nine meals besides the family

October 13—Picked apples from three Smith cider trees and one Ben Davis tree.

November 1—Mother and Papa moved into a little house they had bought in Escondido.

These few notes in my journal completed the 1921 records:

MY JOURNAL ENTRIES 1922

JANUARY

New Year's Day—Sunday, Palomar Mountain, Planwydd. After a long, long lapse, I will try keeping this diary again. Too busy with a hotel! We had a lovely New Year's Day. Another storm began. We had twenty-seven inches of rain practically within ten days that included Christmas. Jack is reading and Catherine very happy with her many new gifts. Resolutions.

Still stormy. It began to snow today. Baked bread.

Beautiful snow world. Mr. Jolly didn't get here. No doubt, the river is too high again. Agnes and George Mendenhall had lunch with us and quite a visit. We enjoy their company so much. Jack helped me house clean.

Today we went horseback to the Mendenhalls and had dinner with Agnes and George. Hap and Charlie were there too. Catherine and I held Jack's horse while he hunted. The game act as if another storm is coming. Streams pouring along and snow on ground—beautiful. Catherine went with Gus to his traps. Wind and fog tonight.

This morning we woke to find fresh snow. Package came from Wales.

Mr. Jolly came late in snowstorm. Agnes and Marion, Stanley and Dickie called while waiting for him. Over six inches in snow today. We made ice cream, using icicles for the freezing. Jack and Gus went hunting. No luck. Wind and fog tonight.

Catherine and I went horseback with Jack to sawmill on an errand. Lovely ride over snow. Agnes, George and Dick Mendenhall were here for lunch. Gus went to Pala for coal oil.

Wild wind. Jack and Gus worked on barn repairing. I arranged my writing affairs in a more orderly way, and I used the typewriter to copy verses, etc. Getting some ready to send off. George and Dick had lunch with us. In the evening Kenneth Spencer, another boy, and Mrs. Beach appeared. They had walked from where their auto was stuck near Lone Fir. Saw to their supper and beds.

Two days since the storm, and the wind has calmed. I took advantage of sunshine by washing clothes. Jack skinned a badger Gus had caught in a trap. He had another fox, too, and two foxes yesterday.

Sunday—Particularly fine day. We all went by wagon to end of lower Doane Valley and brought back two fine metates. I have seen Indian teepees and nearby boulders with as many as twenty metate holes that they used for grinding the acorns. Gus looked after his traps and Jack hunted. Catherine and I strolled and played. Valley is green, streams large. Still lots of snow but the day was warm and most lovely.

By Thursday, we have about six inches of new snow. In the midst of most beautiful snowstorm, we left in car. Were stuck for almost three hours in ditch at foot of mountain. Bitter cold night, the coldest in years. On the lower elevations in the fruit groves, we traveled through areas of heavy smudging, where they are using oil-burning heaters to prevent frost from destroying the fruit. We also had a sandstorm to go through. Routed out folks at Pomona at 1:00 a.m.!

Back on Palomar. It was so lovely to be with my dear parents and Aunt Mamie on her birthday, January 20th. Mother had a splendid birthday dinner to celebrate Aunt Mamie's and my birthday together. The following day we returned home. Tire chains broke on the grade in snow delaying us over and over. Mr. Morgan looked after mail.

Jack went to Pauma Creek, the weir, and Doane Valley to look after gas company interests. While Jack was riding, Gus helped me wash clothes, then fog came up and in the evening, it turned to rain. Happy.

Fresh snow, this morning, but sunshine. Clouded up later and began to snow at nightfall. Dick Mendenhall came and played with Catherine.

Sunday—Snowing all day. Glad we brought up extra supply of fresh vegetables. Mr. Jolly brought fresh meat yesterday.

January 30th—Terrific blizzard overnight and again today. We have twenty-six inches of snow. Jack says he never saw such an ice-blizzard in the far north of Canada. Gus says he never saw such a one in the Swiss Alps in nineteen years. Trails obliterated. Went to the ram and I am worn out. Screaming wind tore off part of our roof.

By today, the weather has half cleared. Catherine and I went to the Point where wild wind blew the snow, thirty-three inches in places, into drifts five or six feet deep. Glorious.

FEBRUARY

Too much snow for Mr. Jolly to deliver mail, but some neighbors came.

We are still snowbound!

Finally, we have mail for first time in ten days. Mr. Hill came and told of stabbing of Kenneth Beach. It has started to rain. Heard that one of my stories accepted by "Primary Plans."

Now we have heavy rain. I did some writing, which I surely enjoy.

Gus worked on phone line again. The river high from rain. Mr. Jolly did not come.

We heard of serious illness of Mrs. Theo Bailey. Foggy, and snow is melting and it is good to be seeing the ground again in places!

Mid-February and Jack began pruning seven trees. Jack & Catherine found the first flower, a filaree.

Heard yesterday of Mrs. Theo Bailey's death. Jack pruned sixteen trees in the yard. Lovely sunshine, and Catherine and I walked to the Point. Jack shod three horses. Mended, including a mattress. I appreciate that I have more vim now than I did a few days ago.

Sunday—We have a beautiful bright morning and happy. We all went horseback over the snow to Silvercrest and then by trail to Boucher's. I used my typewriter while Jack made candy. We have some fog.

Rain and plenty of it today. Glad for a chance to do some extra cleaning and sorting. I am also doing some writing.

Day of rain followed by a day of snow. Mr. Jolly did not get here with the mail. About twenty inches snow this storm. Mr. Morgan called. I helped Gus with some grammar and definitions.

Rain and snow again. A good deal of typing and baking of bread accomplished today.

Sunday—Catherine and I had baths and washed our hair despite weather! Raining hard tonight. I wrote six letters. Jack occupied by reading books by the dozens these stormy weeks and months.

Snowing heavily again. Catherine played in the snow.

Our phone is out of order so Gus went to mend it. Five McClards for dinner and overnight, on their way, they hope, to San Diego. Shoveling snow and using team with car.

MARCH

We are in Perris. Decided to try our luck horseback on regular grade. As the McClards went with auto, we planned to go from the foot of the grade with them to a stage line. However, in half a day they could get only around a few curves from here with their car. The horses floundered to their knees and bodies in snow. Gave up and came back to the house just as the phone rang. Papa was at Rincon waiting for Catherine and me. So, we went horseback to Potrero where he met us. Catherine and I left in the Ford with them and came here. We girls talk and talk! Tomorrow we go on to Pomona. I plan to be away from Palomar for several weeks.

We had breakfast, shopping and lunch in Riverside, and then we came on to Pomona. I miss Mother who is still helping Alice, but glad to be with others.

On Saturday, Papa called for us, bringing Mother, whom I was ever so glad to see. She has Alice's little Beatrice, whom mother has for a week to help Alice after the flu.

Sunday—Looked like rain, and I am afraid of crowds anyway because of the prevalence of flu, so did not go to church.

Aunt Mamie and I took Catherine and Beatrice to a park, where they played on the grass, watched goldfish etc. Very pleasant, and I imagined what it would be like to live in a city. Palomar is better than any park! Enjoying the family, lovely to be with my own parents and Aunt Mamie.

Sunday—After three weeks of visiting family and being away, we are home. Palomar Mountain. Home! Surely good to be home again. Feel much better and very happy. Catherine enjoys her playroom, the sleeping porch Jack enlarged beautifully while we were gone.

He finished pruning orchards on this place on March 25. Gus is still hauling hay from the Salmons, now getting better trail through snow. I helped Gus with a letter in the evening.

Gus plowed the kitchen garden, Jack raked yard, pruned rose bushes. The Morgan family called. Jack & Gus got the McClards' car out of the road, stuck for four weeks.

March 31—Catherine's fourth birthday. Made birthday cake trimmed in red with red candles. Catherine says, "I glory with fun!"

APRIL

Mendenhall children and Catherine at log cabin—Planwydd

On this first day of April, I cleaned house and got a birthday dinner for Catherine. Dick and Leona Mendenhall came to the party, ten miles (twenty in all) horseback and six-year-old Bertha Morgan walked. A real party, Catherine was wild with joy. She and I walked part way home with Bertha in the fog.

April 18—Jack left for Aunt Mamie, bringing her back from Ethanac in car to Doane Road, then wagon. Good to have her home. Two forest service men overnight.

April 21—All of us went for picnic to the hill near Boucher's, men working on the phone line. We found blossoms. Rested, read, and walked. Crab apples seem almost ready to bloom.

(The summer workload again defeated my good intentions to journal regularly and for the remainder of 1923 I only entered brief notes.)

July 29—We had about forty-two guests for the weekend.

Aug. 14—Alice and I went with family and guests for a picnic breakfast in Doane Valley, eighteen of us. Left here at 5:20 a.m. We had a fine breakfast of steak and toast over coals. Coffee and cantaloupe too.

9

Planwydd Hired Help—the Odd, and the Delightful

My Limerick Place Cards for Hired Help

Jack Roberts is acting tonight as your host,
And says to you now in a most hearty toast:
Here's to you all! May no apple fall
And strike on your head e'er
you leave for the coast.

The little aunt who sits here
Has always been known as a dear.
She will never grow old, but often has told
Twenty-five is her limit each year.

Here is Elsie the cook, you can tell at a look,
With flour on her hands and
her nose in a book.
You can tell her afar, wherever you are;
For the odor of onions and
grease ain't mistook.

This is the baby, so funny and fair,
Who rules like a queen from
her little highchair.
She reaches for things and
jabbers and sings.

But all of all our friends are
polite and don't care.

Here sits a man who is called just Slim.
"Mr. Holmes" is another name for him.
Alas! His fate perchance may be
To grow so fat he can hardly see.

Mr. Millman may seem still,
But he lends a hand with a right good will.
Gathering apples is now his fate.
But in after years he'll
have pomp and state.

The gentleman here is called Bill Beach
Who packs the apples the other men reach.
In the future a blond Mrs. Beach I see,
But oh, bow—legged as she can be!

For Mr. Webb this place is laid —
He takes the apples down the grade.
His fortune then at last shall be
To own all the trucks in the whole county

My diary entries for 1923 were totally neglected. It was a year filled with guests at the resort and the hiring and firing of resort workers. It was an eclectic bunch of apple pickers and household help necessary for the operation of both the ranch and the resort. Their extremes of background, expectations, and former positions created endless possibilities for disasters or delight. Jack preferred British cooks that he hired through a San Diego employment agency. The British were accustomed to large households with a hierarchy of staff. Mountain hired help often became more like family friends and there was little attention paid to social order.

Some of our problems with hired help at our informal little summer resort and apple ranch seem amusing now more than a half-century later. Back then, when the forests were greener and the distant views clearer, the mountain was wilder and more isolated. Not everyone who came to the mountain embraced it as we did. One cook was with us only a few days.

"I'd stay if there was only a movie up here," she explained, "or sidewalks, so I could go for a walk."

The old Indian woman who came up from a reservation at the foot of the mountain as my first assistant stayed for even less time. Santos, the Spaniard or Mexican who was building the simple one-room cottages we were preparing as bedrooms for our first opening, had suggested that she would be good help. But she spoke no English, and I no Spanish! And I certainly spoke no Indian dialect. The only night she was there, I heard her in the kitchen in the wee small hours and went to investigate. By signs, she made me understand that she had a terrible pain and was making a fire in the wood range to get a hot griddle. That was the type of therapy later outmoded by electric heating pads.

Once we had her back in bed, I feared she was dying. Jack hastily summoned Santos from his bedroom in the part of the barn, which at one time had been the only dwelling house on the ranch. Santos told us she was really the mother of one of his wives! He talked with her gently, said she'd had such attacks before, but drove her home in his buggy the next day.

We later tried a young Indian girl from below, lovely and bright. She had attended the Riverside Sherman Institute for Indians. This school taught agriculture and domestic science to Native American children with a goal to assimilate them into mainstream society. The girl, of course, knew English. That was ostensibly the cause of her early departure. On a weekend busy with many guests, when I particularly needed her, she abruptly announced that she had to go home immediately for a day or so, as she had remembered that she had to write a letter for her father. We knew that there was an Indian fiesta in progress near the foot of the mountain, and we surmised she had thought up an alibi for attending it. Without fail, whenever there was a fiesta nearby, she would want to leave. Of course, it was always on a weekend, our rush times! Exit Victoria. Also, exit with her, a little sister who had come up with her and was really very useful in the kitchen, young as she was. "I've washed dishes all my life," she explained.

We needed helpers not only for the resort, but also in the apple season. For several years, when Jack leased all available orchards on the mountain, we needed a big crew of pickers and packers each fall. The Webb brothers of Escondido hauled the filled boxes in large trucks. The first year (1918), the workers in the orchards were Indians from below the mountain.

In those days, Louis Salmons ordinarily directed the annual spring repairs to the grade. One year Jack was in charge instead, with a crew of Indians. Otherwise, it was only at first that we employed mainly Indians. So many young men had gone off to war.

Though there would be a foreman, Jack supervised everything. The men were an odd group—some strays, some illiterate, some very knowledgeable. One fall, the foreman was a former high school teacher or principal. A foreman must be kept happy, if possible. This pleasant older man had said he would like applesauce for breakfast every morning. That sounded easy, on an apple ranch, and I saw to it that there was always some on hand for him. Except once when as we were serving I realized there was none. None in the pantry or Mexican cooler. I still remember my regret in opening a jar of it that I had canned, when loaded apple trees surrounded the house.

We had briefly a songwriter who entertained us one evening with some of his music. As I recall, it wasn't as delightful an evening as we had hoped! I remember on a Sunday evening playing old hymns on the little schoolhouse organ we had acquired when the school building was sold. Any pickers interested joined us in singing.

Usually Jack hired all help through a San Diego employment agency—apple pickers as well as a summer cook and waitresses who also served as chambermaids. My cousin Sadie, who was companionable and a joy, did come up again to be a help and assist me in whatever need. And sometimes I had friends working in the kitchen.

Altogether, during those five years on the ranch we had a variety of kitchen helpers. One fall apple season we had two cooks and two dishwashers. One spring, I wrote to my old friend the Dean of Women at Pomona College to ask if she knew of two college girls there who would like to work for me the coming summer. The two who came were Bethel, whose father was a very well-to-do farmer in the Midwest, and Lois, educated in Switzerland. Her father was Minister Plenipotentiary to Albania. They were charming girls, willing workers though they knew practically nothing about housework. They were waitresses, dishwashers, and chambermaids. The guests were delighted with them. But the current cook, Mrs. Miller, very English, could not appreciate them. She was accustomed to work in an English household where there were seventeen servants. In those days when servants were servants with their own ranks of butler, housekeeper, cook, etc. and much above the mere maids, she could not endure our casual democratic way of life.

The guests were charmed by Bethel and Lois and treated them as equals. But Mrs. M. felt that as maids, they were far beneath her. She knew her own place, way down below the guests. How could the guests treat those girls as equals? She was pathetically jealous of them. We had explained that we didn't want tips given at our little *all in the family* resort. But Mrs. M, accustomed to being one of a line of servants wait-

Top—Planwydd staff on horseback—including Catherine
Right—Elsie on her mountain

ing expectantly, almost held her hand out ready whenever a guest was departing.

Mrs. M. never forgot her place. When we had dinner served picnic style on Inspiration Point, I told her she was to sit on the ground with the rest of us and only to help pass things around. It was almost more than she could bear.

At one meal, when luncheon guests had left the room and only the family table was still occupied, she came in from the kitchen, and as always stood quietly waiting to speak until she was noticed. I can still see her subservient attitude and hear her low differential voice.

"Excuse me, Mrs. Roberts, your house is on fire."

As nothing about her suggested that this was a fact, I couldn't take it in at first. "What did you say?" I asked.

She repeated it, quiet, unemotional, as befitted a servant. To her obvious horror, I did not act as the dignified lady of the house should. I yelped and sprang up and raced for the kitchen. It was true. The kitchen roof was blazing, though already Jack and Gus had it under control.

She was shocked that I dressed Catherine, then about three, in a manner I considered appropriate for the mountain. She played under the apple trees all day. She wore coveralls, little gingham dresses, and similar outfits. Mrs. M. had a child of her own now being boarded somewhere. At least once Mrs. M said softly, no doubt troubled by seeming to disapprove of anything her mistress did, but unable to keep silence any longer, "My little girl always wears white."

Miss Kendall was another cook we had one summer. She was a bewildering character, very proud of the fact that in World War I she had been a clerk. She had a magnificent cloak of navy blue. She was a tall, large, stately woman, who of her own desire, always wore at her work crisp white uniforms. She sent them down the mountain to be laundered.

Our informality and lack of a caste system shocked her. She could not tolerate Ruth and Frenchy, a young married couple who, in what she considered an inferior position, worked for us at the same time. Unfortunately, they had the bedroom next to hers, and Miss K. complained to me that she heard undesirable things she should not be expected to hear. Suddenly this situation came to a head. She fairly demanded that the couple be discharged. Jack refused to fire them. They were good workers in the orchards and as servers. The cook became so difficult that we asked her to leave. Instead, she became violent. I am not sure whether we had asked her to leave or she announced ahead of us that she was going. I have often wondered if she might not have been an addict who ran out of dope. Whatever the cause, her final fury was terrifying. She demanded arrogantly that she be driven down the mountain. Jack knew he needed to go to San Diego for another cook. Though Jack was usually ready to go to any trouble to help anyone stranded up there, he told her coldly she could go down with the Bailey stage that would be leaving Sunday morning.

At her request, Jack had earlier taken her trunk down for repairs, which required that it be left there. Now she insisted that she could not leave without it. It must be brought up for her. We suggested emergency cartons. She met with supreme scorn our suggestions for the emergency cartons, which she eventually used. She shut herself into her room and refused to come out for meals. Even when it was little Catherine who tapped on her door to say that a meal was ready she ignored the invitation.

Once when I, in a determinedly friendly tone, suggested through the closed door that she join us for dinner, her choked and her violent tone was terrifying.

"It would choke me. It would kill me to eat your food!"

However, there were indications that she had slipped out to the kitchen for some nourishment those two nights before Sunday. At night, I heard her pacing the floor in her room. I shouldn't have been at all surprised if she had crept into our bedroom bent on murder. It was a strenuous weekend with guests, including Judge and Mrs. Cary who came repeatedly and became our real friends. With Ruth and Jack to help me, and Aunt Mamie looking after Catherine, I managed meals and all.

Sunday morning before the stage was due, I saw through the window stately Miss K. in her handsome uniform cloak, head high, face cold and white. Judge Cary happened to overhear her raving against us to some of these people.

He stepped into sight and said, "Young woman, I don't know who you are. But do you know that you could be arrested for these lies you are telling about these people?"

Afterwards the stage driver said she kept saying such things to the other passengers that he finally told her that if she didn't stop those lies, he'd stop the stage and leave her alone on the mountain grade many miles from anywhere.

After the weekend guests had left, we went down ourselves to a San Diego hotel for overnight. At the employment agency early the next morning, the manager said she had already been there maligning us. He said he told her that he had for a long time sent us many employees, apple pickers, resort workers, and had never before heard a word against us, and that he was going to blackball her so that she could never get another job in Southern California.

Mildred was another cook who had pride in her status. She was indeed a character. She was red haired, temperamental, and superstitious. She had worked as a barmaid in a Nevada mining town and later as manager of a hotel there. Mildred looked down upon Mrs. J., a brilliant and highly educated female guest who stayed on helping with various chores and became a friend. When Mrs. J., in our rush of work, helped with the laundry, Mildred condescendingly called her "the wash lady." Mildred raved to me about an elderly guest who came late to dinner one evening and asked her to clean and cook the quail he had just shot. She was outraged, muttering about "the pest." But in cleaning the bird, she found he had tucked a one-dollar bill inside its cavity, and her anger changed to delight.

Poor Mildred! Sometimes her superstitions really troubled her. There was the gorgeous moonlight evening when she, Mrs. J., and I went up to our Inspiration Point above the orchard to enjoy more fully the full moon over the forest. As we sat on the boulders overlooking what seemed like the whole world below, Mrs. J. told us fascinating tales of some of her own experiences that dealt with incredible and inexplicable facets of the unknown universe. Mildred was so frightened by those stories that she begged Mrs. J. to stop and finally left us rather than hear more. She went alone by the wooded trail back to the house.

Somehow, Mildred felt virtuous and superior because she had not smoked, unlike some of the women in the mining town. She must have had a bad inferiority complex for she seemed to feel it essential to express her superiority. She addressed me as her employer as "Lady."

She was a great talker. She talked scornfully of her British husband. The last straw was when he, a Britisher, left his boots outside the bedroom door for her to clean.

Mildred boasted often of a gentleman from Alaska, her "hero," as she called him. He had written her that he would come up to see her on July 4. She fumed, fretted, and finally raged when the day wore on and passed without him. Then around noon the next day, he came to the gate almost staggering, and she ran into his arms. He said he had taken a bus to bring him as near to our unfamiliar mountain as possible, then thought he'd hike up by what he thought would be a short cut through a canyon. He spent the night in the depths, ate the chocolate he'd been bringing her, and finally managed to climb out in the morning. An arrangement was made as Jack needed an extra hired man just then, so the "hero" stayed awhile, telling almost incredible tales of the frontier.

When I offered to help Mildred clean chickens, she tossed her head and said in anger, "It would be a favor for you not to help."

Mildred was with us for at least a part of two seasons. The morning she was leaving, she was in such a temper that when a breakfast guest asked for more coffee she said there was none – a really ridiculous lie. And yet, I was rather fond of Mildred. At least, life was never dull in her vicinity.

Once we had in the kitchen an inexperienced girl who assured me she wanted to learn, but curiously was too often not in sight when most needed. She flirted with the first guest of the season, a young boarder, who stayed in one of the half-dozen scattered tents that had been added as bedroom cottages. We found her walking in the woods with him while at a particular rush hour, and I had to fire her with regret.

Our hired men, as they used to be called, were seasonal apple pickers—except for the first ones who came to us. The apple pickers and packers from the agency were often characters and usually not well educated. Such a variety we began with, an Indian or two and then our murderer!

Once we employed a large man who looked like a pirate. For obvious reasons among ourselves, we called him Silver Bracelet because of the ornament on his wrist. He had been a sailor and seemed well decorated with tattoos. He was entranced with our little Catherine, then about three, and said he was going to leave her a chest full of treasures collected on his far travels. That never materialized.

One night we did think might be his last. He was suddenly extremely ill, probably with pneumonia. Jack got the poor delirious fellow into the car and drove him to the county hospital in San Diego the same night. When Jack got safely back the next morning he said that on the way down that awful west grade, so narrow and winding, with the precipices at the side, Silver Bracelet was so wild with delirium that Jack laid a monkey wrench where he could instantly grab it. He said if necessary, he would have knocked his passenger out rather than have him seize the wheel or attack Jack and send them both hurtling over the edge.

The fall that Sadie was with us, we also employed a friend from Arizona, Martha Stanley. She was a stout, friendly girl whose constant cheerfulness as well as her service, was especially appreciated by at least one of the pickers. He was an elderly man who had a standard morning greeting for her when she came smiling into the dining room with steaming breakfast dishes.

"Thank God for Martha!" he would say devoutly.

He was a remarkable person. He seemed to know anything and everything. No matter what subject came up, he was ready to give a little lecture about it—to the bewilderment of most of his listeners. He said that every year he went here and there picking various fruits in their seasons. Then in winter, he took a room in a cheap San Diego hotel, used his summer and fall savings, and lived in the big city library.

Up on our mountain, with no chances to go down, the pickers could hardly have spent the money they were earning. I wonder how they kept contented with so little to entertain them. One fall, we did give them a party that provided a lot of fun, at least for Martha, Sadie, and me. It was a surprise Halloween dinner—a surprise in more ways than one.

Sometimes, if not always, we took a big meal at noon to whatever orchard was being used that day, where perhaps we would join them for a picnic. That day, with the house entirely to ourselves, we decorated it lavishly. Branches of golden oak leaves and rosy sprays of Dogwood were a background. I had some construction paper with which we cut out such appropriate items as cats and witches on broomsticks and tacked them to the walls. We wrote out individual menus, partly humorous, largely in French, indicating that the usually informal meal would be served in as many courses as possible. We made place cards with a personal rhyme to fit each man. Then we prepared a special dinner. We chuckled over everything in anticipation of the surprise.

When the men came in to dinner, they stared about at the decorated walls and table and then sat down, startled to find the place cards and menus. Probably a number of them had never heard of such things, much less seen them. They were silent, looking embarrassed. And why wasn't everything served at once? The courses, one after another, bewildered them further. Our greatest fun had been in planning the entrée, or what appeared to be the entrée. With an air, Martha brought in a large serving platter with a great rounded oval cover I had inherited, designed to keep a roast hot. She set it down at the head of the table, lifted the cover, and out sprang a very live and very angry black cat! The response was not the shout of laughter we had happily anticipated, but more disgust, or pity for our unbalanced minds. At least the steak that followed was very welcome, as was finally the big cake. Anyway, we girls had fun.

Mealtimes occasionally resulted in actual drama. I remember the young chap, Ray, who one morning at breakfast got a fish bone from smoked herring, stuck in his throat. He was taken to Pala on horseback to the reservation doctor who, unable to take it out, pushed it further down.

Once while Catherine was still a baby, we temporarily had with us another young fellow whose family we knew slightly. When Jack had business in San Diego that would keep him away overnight, he felt safe, if leaving me with the young baby, because this boy would be on the place, sleeping in the regular living quarters for the men that had been built for that purpose in a part of the excellent barn—stable. A horse had died (or by necessity been shot) and because of the cold weather with snow on the ground Jack thought he could be cremated. The young chap was busy all day cutting and piling brush over the animal and then burning it. A spooky sort of atmosphere!

I knew the boy admired me and the obvious extent of this troubled me, as it is not uncommon for a youth's first love to be an older woman. At dusk, he filled the wood box to the brim, kept asking if there wasn't something else he could do for me, and after dinner loitered in the kitchen while I washed the dishes. He began looking at me in a way no woman could misinterpret. I finally got rid of him, and I went to my bedroom with the baby and the dog. That door had no lock, but I barricaded it, kept the easily accessible window closed and locked, blew out the lamp, and slipped into bed, with the baby beside me and the dog at my feet. Would the young dog, if necessary, try to protect me from someone he also knew? As the night went on, my terror grew. There were few people on the mountain in winter and the snow was fairly deep. I thought if I heard him trying to break in at either window I'd slip out of the other and run with the baby to the nearest neighbor, at the old Cleaver place, perhaps a mile away. I wondered if I could run over the snow with the baby. I listened and prayed and nothing happened. But I will never forget my desperate fear of that long winter night and until Jack came home the next day.

Charlie Stoessel, from Alsace Lorraine, was with us perhaps a year and a half. We liked and appreciated him. Then came Gus Weber, from Switzerland, who stayed with us for it must have been two or three years, until we left. He was also at the place later, too, finally going to work for the Forest Service, then newly established on the mountain, and later for many years at the Observatory after it came to the mountain. He was a handsome young fellow much admired by the girls. He was our right-hand man and indispensable. He did a thousand things besides his ranch work. He kept my big wood box always full, turned the crank of our old-fashioned washing machine, and helped to keep guests happy. Gus also often entertained us with his yodeling.

Gus particularly loved Aunt Mamie, always adored by everyone. I did get tired of providing three big meals a day, on time, year in and year out, even on holidays. Sometimes on winter Sundays, when the snow fell steadily and no outsider came near, I would think if we didn't have a hired man I could, once in a while, serve a late breakfast or a light pickup supper. But we couldn't get along without Gus, so pleasant and friendly as well as efficient. I wish I could hear again on a moonlit night his beautiful yodeling from somewhere off in the woods.

When some of the guests wanted a horse saddle trip, Gus had the horses ready and, if wanted, went as a guide. He loved Catherine, then age two to four. He liked to take her to the pasture, high on his shoulders, when he went to milk the two Jersey cows. And she thought it great fun when he told her to stand still while he sent a spurt of milk straight from the cow into her mouth. Catherine often ran through the orchard picking up apples, eating a few bites and throwing them down. To her delight, there were always plenty of apples and she had all of the milk she wanted. I didn't worry much if she refused carrots or spinach.

When autumn came and guests were rare, we still needed the extra help until after the apple season, but they were apt to be of a different type, more informal, sometimes old friends. That was fun, especially when I would be chief cook myself. There were emergencies when Jack and I both cooked.

My dear friend Edna Roof was with me one summer, and another teacher friend Mary Maynard helped another summer. I especially enjoyed the times my cousin Sadie Hayes was one of our workers.

Aunt Mamie was both family and like a private Nanny for Catherine. She helped in so many ways. Aunt Mamie would often read aloud under the lilac trees while all darned stockings. Aunt Mamie once came back from the spring with a rattlesnake over her walking stick. It had become a fad to use rattlesnake skins for belts and hatbands. Knowing her brother would skin it for her, Aunt Mamie had been on the lookout for a snake. They always kept a rattlesnake remedy on hand. Alonzo skinned rattlesnakes until he heard of a man poisoned through his hands.

Though the years were full of work, we enjoyed our surroundings, often relaxing with books and the many enjoyable outings around the mountain.

As Catherine grew older, she almost became a part of the staff. One guest signed the guest book, "Let Catherine May be your guide." Indeed, Catherine often acted as a guide to guests. They delighted in seeing how she believed in fairies and loved Faerie Wood. Once we had a rather pompous opera singer pausing for effect during a moonlight program. Catherine piped up. "Mamie, do coyotes have hearts like a chicken?" That took the wind out of the opera singer's performance.

10

The Roaring Twenties and Beyond 1924-1946

Haunted Memories of Palomar
By Elsie Roberts - 1935

There are those who fear shapes in the darkness,
Those who tremble at dream visitations—
Ah, but I—I am haunted by beauty,
When the past and absent are present,
And with magic of memory mountains
Far away, long unseen, rise about me.
In the blackness of night, tossing, sleepless,
(Then when all things are hidden, and seen, too)
Or perchance it may be at mid-morning,
As from prosaic floors dust is garnered,
They are there: sudden, vivid, a vision.
Autumn leaves on a trail that winds, climbing,
High above, swaying evergreen branches;
Shining vistas of breath-taking grandeur,
Frail wild flowers by waterfalls nodding.
I hear birdcalls and wind in the forest,
Catch the tang and fragrance of mountains.
What a boon, to be haunted by beauty!

Catherine turned five in 1923. It seemed to be the time for us to begin making plans to move back to town to enable her to have an education and childhood friendships. Moving to the city for the sake of our only daughter was perhaps similar to moving from Virginia for the sake of Gilman's health. I once again left behind much that I loved. For the sake of Catherine, we would go down the mountain and begin a new life in the city.

Jack still had grand plans for success on Palomar. He hoped to build a lodge unlike any ever imagined for our quiet, unpretentious mountain community. He had a number of contacts with influential men in San Diego and Los Angeles.

San Diego had much to offer in way of restaurants, concerts, fabulous weather, and endless possibilities for Jack to succeed in real estate. Our city by the sea was growing and the country was prosperous.

Jack exercised his charismatic personality in selling real estate. I hired weekly household help and learned to drive. I cut my hair in a bob and marceled it in the style of the day. Indeed, we had jumped from quiet mountain life into the roaring twenties. My love of literature and writing continued, in writing short stories for children's publications. My journal reminds me of that first year down the mountain.

My Journal 1924

JANUARY

New Year's Day 1924—We are renting 4800 Panorama Dr., San Diego, a large home in the prestigious University Heights neighborhood, overlooking the steep Mission Valley Canyon. It is glorious to be perched on the edge of the canyon. Gus Weber is helping me develop a lovely garden down the steep slope. Agnes and George Mendenhall, Gus Weber, and Mrs. Willie staying here and Mrs. Jackson and the five Pickerells came for dinner. We received a ten-pound turkey.

This first week in January, we left about 6:30 a.m. Friday in our lovely new Willys Knight Sedan. I went to see Alice's house and Papa's lots in Pomona. Aunt Mamie and I went to see West of the Water Tower at the beautiful new California Theater. Ernest came from Monrovia last night where he is now doing singing and evangelistic work.

Jack Roberts

Sunday we returned home. We enjoyed dinner at Murrieta enroute. We had much pleasure in seeing the folks, but I do love my new home. Gus is working on trails in the canyon. Jack went up to Palomar and came back with two quail.

We went to hear John Phillip Sousa and his band at the Spreckels Theatre January 12. Wonderful! Gus Weber working for us again.

I finished making about eighteen glasses of marmalade. We went to a Japanese garden in Old Town for plants. We had a picnic lunch in the canyon. Jack took us to the Savoy Club in the evening.

On January 25, I took my first real lesson to learn to drive our car. I have made a list of fourteen rules to start the car. Trying to remember all of them and learning to shift gears. Made myself an additional list of five rules to stop the car.

I had a driving lesson in the morning. Aunt Mamie, Catherine, and I went for a matinee to see the Russian ballerina Anna Pavlova and her ballet. Wonderful! I read this is to be Anna Pavlova's last American tour.

FEBRUARY

Elated that I received word that Junior Home Magazine has accepted my story "Turkey Gobblers and Hens" at one cent a word. Another auto lesson for me. Jack went to Tijuana on business.

Pomona—I left home about 7 a.m. and got here about noon. Papa is very sick. Hylinda, her children Sam and Sarah are here. Alice's new home is three blocks away. I stay at night with her.

I walked downtown to do errands for mother and hunt for things to tempt Papa's appetite. Read aloud to Papa. Absalom came for Hylinda, and Sam and Sarah went back with him.

As Papa had a bad night, Uncle Douglas drove me to Claremont where I talked with Dr. Staughton about Papa and called on the doctor's wife. I have been friends with them for years at Pomona College. He came here later and made a thorough examination. Doctor says it is heart trouble.

One week later and Papa's condition remains no better. I read to Papa, cleaned house. Alice and I did errands together downtown—like old times.

MARCH

March 2—Papa delirious more than before. Doctor came and said it might be clot on the brain so we are anxious in a new way.

It is a day later and Papa better, clearer mind, so we are very grateful. I have been here two weeks, and I am going home again. We brought Beatrice back for a few weeks; she and Catherine were good on the way. Alice is anticipating the birth of her fifth child in the next couple of weeks. Beatrice and Catherine are very happy together. Beatrice is four now, so quite good with Catherine. Catherine goes well on skates now and Beatrice has Catherine's old tricycle that Jack mended for her. It keeps Catherine happier to have Beatrice to play with. I wonder more again about adopting a child.

Mid-March and I went out three times in the car, had my first experience getting gas! Enjoying it. We revel in the canyon; and I do enjoy working in it. Beauty of nature!

We heard later that Malcolm was born to Alice today, March 16. Alice now has five children under the age of nine years old, thankful I can help her with Beatrice. I made cookies for the children and a cake with Swans Down cake flour.

March 18—Papa has died, and we are missing his presence in our lives. I am numb with grief.

A week later none of us very energetic still. We keep receiving letters of sympathy and that helps a lot. I am trying to help mother with bank papers. Somehow, the days go by in a daze. Mother is wonderful! I cannot realize dear Papa is gone, but it comes in pangs.

Mother has been here with us, but she left early for Pomona to help the housekeeper care for Alice's other children that are suffering with measles. Poor Alice is still in Alhambra

Alonzo & May Hayes

with her new baby. Now Catherine shows signs of getting measles. We are to keep Beatrice and Catherine apart.

Catherine broke out with the surest signs of measles on her birthday, March 31! What a month in our family! Dear Papa is now gone and Alice's little Malcolm born. Beatrice broke out with measles. Quarantine sign put up. New regulations require us to report measles and post a quarantine sign on the front door. Now the two children are in bed together, thinking it rather fun, sitting up and playing with the bed table Jack had arranged. Gus appeared for lunch, and I showed him how the canyon has come on.

APRIL

Mrs. Wood, as usual, is coming to clean this week, etc. She's a prize. Miss Sweetwood called, and we talked of Williams, Arizona. The children have a lively time in bed. Miss Hauser (the dog), was taken to Palomar by Gus to avoid rabies. They put poison out for dogs. Also, miss our dear "Kitty Toots" who died, evidently of poison. We are trying to keep that news from Catherine.

Papa gone three weeks, and I can't realize it!

Mrs. Wood came to stay with Aunt Mamie and children this evening while Jack and I went to dinner given for resort people at the San Diego Hotel. Pleasant time with music, speeches, etc. Then all went to Balboa Theater to see _A Man's a Man_.

Children still need to stay indoors. No sunshine. They're good about it, but often cross. Planted dahlias and transplanted cosmos. Mrs. Wood came and I did extra straightening while she cleaned and did extra cooking.

Mid-April and Quarantine has been lifted! Packed Beatrice's things and went with Jack to take her home. We brought mother home with us. Mother is wonderful and brave always. Mr. McBride is working for us on the garden. Mrs. Wood cleans for me.

End of April able to take Catherine and Anne to the zoo for lunch and walked about and then to the Natural History Museum.

MAY

Jack took Catherine to First of May Frolic at La Mesa Country Club. I am enjoying outings in the car. I went with Jack to luncheon of Mountain Resorts Association at San Diego Hotel. We enjoyed an evening of vaudeville at Pantages.

We took a trip with Jack and had a picnic lunch in Julian. Looking over manuscripts.

Palomar on May 24th—Mrs. Jackson came early, we met the Roberts family, and two cars went to Palomar. Lunch at Uncle Nate's, and we stayed in the log cabin for the night. I particularly think of dear Papa here. Very lovely spring beauty. The men got fish from Doane Valley; we went part way and walked back by Wonder Trail, blue violets and dogwood. Sunset at the point.

Sunday—Sunrise at Inspiration Point. Mrs. Roberts and two older girls and I walked to Baileys for her to call on her friend there. Lovely day, Jack gathered rhubarb. Lunch at Mendenhalls. We were home by eight p.m. with a snake for the zoo. Palomar meant much.

JUNE

Made Rhubarb Cobbler. We left early and had a picnic at Monument Beach, on the border of Mexico. Catherine played in the sand.

Took Catherine to visit schools, and then registered her at Normal.

Sunday—I taught Sunday school while Jack drove to Julian.

Cut out endless pictures for scrapbooks for Ellis Island children. Catherine read to me, early lessons we both love. Jack took us to Chula Vista. Shopped and visited the library

Mother, Alice, Ernest and their five children came for a few days June 20. All of us drove to Tijuana in the afternoon.

Ernest sang twice at a Christian church. I looked after Gilman aged nearly two while others are at the service.

Alice and her family left June 24. Mother is staying here. House put to rights. Mrs. Jackson for lunch, and we all drove with Jack to El Cajon.

Catherine and I went to Palomar June 25 with Jack and Capt. Bradshaw and his little son. We enjoyed dinner at our place on Palomar. It looks fine as a resort, kept by the Tuckers. Gathered azaleas and larkspurs.

Van Nuys Hotel, Los Angeles June 28—all of us left at noon, left mother at Alice's in Pomona, and the rest of us are tired out, came to hotel for the night. Jack to stay on here while others of us visit.

Sunday, Long Beach June 29—We took Aunt Mamie to Hylinda's home where she is to stay for now. Mother met us there. Delightful, old-time large family supper. So good to be here and to go with Ivy Harnett to new St. Luke's for the evening service!

Los Angeles June 30—Ivy bobbed my hair off! Then we came to meet Jack. We are all disappointed to have mortgage given us instead of cash.

JULY

Had lunch at Hylinda's. Alice and family were there. Mr. Allen took us to the Encino Country Club, wonderful place, with banquet for a Chamber of Commerce, and overnight here.

Fourth of July with lunch on the strand. We drove to Coronado by ferry, then around by the strand, to the Mexican border and then home. Jack set off neighborhood fireworks. I feel bad not to have money for mother from the sale of the mountain property

We have arranged to send mother $3,100 we owed her. Mr. Tucker from Palomar called. He is the manager for Planwydd and listed as manager for National Forest Country Club.

I weigh ninety-five pounds. I have decided to give myself some "Instructions to Get Fat:"

1. Don't worry

2. Don't talk too much.

3. Get extra sleep.

4. Eat cream, butter, milk, etc., in extra amounts.

5. Drink <u>Bohemian</u>. A non-alcoholic malt tonic advertised as containing "predigested carbohydrates." Whatever that means, at least I began drinking Bohemian.

6. Don't get overtired.

Sunday—Taught primary Sunday school and loved it. Aunt Mamie and I stayed to church. Jack met us and we went to Pacific Beach, picnic lunch. Reread a manuscript.

AUGUST

Hair bob and marcel August 26th. Train to L.A. with Auntie Mamie and Catherine. Bus to mother's and Alice's new homes.

SEPTEMBER

At Mission Beach. Swimming, rowing, and fishing. We caught a shark.

My hair cut again and marceled with little waves just two weeks since the last hair bob. Jack went to Julian.

Took Catherine to enter Garfield School.

OCTOBER

Oct. 12—I decided to keep Catherine from school because of infantile paralysis [polio] outbreak. Drove to tract where Jack has sold more lots than any of the others. Typing stories.

Sunday—Still keeping Catherine from public gatherings. Finished typing another story. We walked to the gardens with the Woods. I feel fortunate to live right next to Mission Cliff Gardens that goes from the other end of our street, Panorama Street to Sixth Street overlooking Mission Valley from the rim of the canyon. This spectacular park covers forty-two acres and includes an ostrich farm, lily pond, lovely flowers and plants.

Catherine back at school October 27th after two weeks out. Jack to Palomar.

NOVEMBER

Nov. 4—I voted for Coolidge. Pantages again in the evening.

Finished typing What's in a Name.

Catherine went to S.S. with Mrs. R. while Jack hunted and brought back quail for dinner.

Made a crossword puzzle myself. They are now very popular. Jack left for Palomar.

Thanksgiving November 27—Jack stayed home. Twenty-three of us are at Mother's home. It is lovely. She is very brave. I made four pies.

I helped mother the day after her big dinner. Went to Hylinda's and discovered she'd bobbed her hair!

I came Home with Cousin Cameron November 29th, bringing Dorothy. Jack is okay. My weight is ninety two pounds.

Enjoyed the zoo with the children.

Town with Jack, then shopping. Again, we went to Pantages in the evening. Stuff dates for sick soldiers and prepare gifts for the poor on December 23rd. We made nine plum puddings.

———

I failed to keep a journal after 1924. I always loved words; suddenly the words churning in my heart collided with a huge dam, and I felt that no longer could they flow in my journal. Life is full of expectations. I became unsure what to do with my expectations.

Now, I need to look back to record for you what happened in those years when my journal became silent. After several miscarriages, my desire became to adopt a child; I did not want Catherine to grow up as an only child. My childhood was so wonderful having sisters and even dear Gilman for the years we had him. I wanted the same for Catherine. Jack seemed to feel having only one child was fine. I often think of how his precious little Welsh mother must have felt, with fading dreams of ever holding her only granddaughter. My heart ached for her. When I was around Alice's happy bunch of five children (eventually she cherished seven), I tried not to feel jealous. I tried. They were such a lively, fun bunch, and Ernest and Alice such wonderful parents.

I enjoyed that first year of life in the city, such excitement. However it seemed I was happiest when creating spots of beauty in the canyon, away from the nightclubs and entertainment Jack enjoyed. I missed the serenity of Palomar and the simple life we had shared there on my mountain. Jack's great plans for Palomar continued for a time.

Somehow, the grand resort he envisioned and produced a brochure for and the architects drawing of such an imposing edifice failed to fit with how I have always loved the feel of the mountain. Sitting on a rock, trekking the trails, exploring and discovering flowers brought me such peace and serenity. Thick walls and "royal grandeur" seemed to me like they would change how closely people could experience God's creation.

The brochures for Jack's dream resort were impressive and though I helped him write the words, they seemed futile. I had wondered if Jack could be content if his dream failed to come about:

Top—Jack's design for lodge.
Right— National Forest
Country Club brochure

Here where the air reverberates with the thrill of enthusiasm,
youth returns to chase away the encroaching streaks of gray and
defies the years to leave their marks. Wildflowers in mature
profusion mingle their varied colors and patterns rare. With
clouds for neighbors and flowers and trees and birds and game
to make the hours all too short, this is indeed a paradise.

The National Forest Country Club is the answer to that
longing for some place to which you might go, and in royal
manner participate in the grandeur that nature ordained, should
be yours to enjoy. This novel club embraces every outdoor
sport in the rough. For the huntsman, the disciple of Isaac

Walton, the horseman, the trail seekers and those who come solely to lounge and rest, there is more than enough amid the exclusiveness of club life to lure you from your routine of usual duties. A mountain paradise a mile high in the clouds.

The clubhouse will include guestrooms, and a complete club service will be maintained at popular prices. Sleeping lodges may be secured. These are to be equipped with fireplaces, and wood supplied for your use, together with modern conveniences.

National Forest Country Club is located on the lofty ridge of Palomar Mountain in San Diego County amid the countryside of which poets have sung their lures and sentiment always waxes warm.

On a site that overlooks the valley a mile below, surrounded by thousands of acres of the Cleveland National Forest, this club holds attractions that the outdoor lover will be quick to appreciate. Even in winter's grasp, the temperate breezes from the ocean, about twenty-eight miles away, make the days delightful. Contrary to most summertime experiences in the mountains, the heat is cooled by the same ozone laden zephyrs.

It is but a five-hour motor ride from Los Angeles and only three hours from San Diego over paved highways and good mountain roads all the way.

A San Diego newspaper account boasted of Jack as a sportsman. Indeed, he loved the out of doors, but it seemed as if he felt the need to impress others.

Jack Roberts. John Planwydd Roberts, that's his full name, but it's been whittled down to Jack Roberts and he's a real sportsman of wide experience. He left Wales and landed in Minneapolis. In Minnesota, he learned how to get the best of a rough grouse and tell the number of feet of lumber in a tall tree. For several years, he was a lumber cruiser in Minnesota. The lumber game has produced some good sportsmen.

Owning a 1200-acre ranch on the shores of Great Slave Lake in Canada, Jack put in some of his time up there where he was known as "The Yankee." Moose, bear, bighorn sheep, wild goats and deer were plentiful, and there he learned the lessons of the open spaces, how to read signs—the art of trailing—and all of the experience that goes to make the most of a man.

Those were happy days for Jack, and he didn't mind being compelled to stay there for a while.

"Small game up there was simply legion," he said in telling of the good things available for the Nimrod and angler. "I have seen ducks, geese, cranes—all the web feet and waders—in immense flocks in the fall of the year, sometimes in clouds. Always the shooting is especially good each fall just before the annual migration begins. The federal migratory treaty between Canada and the United States has been the salvation of the migratory game birds. I've seen it's good."

When the war involved Jack's uncle and the time came to line up, John Planwydd Roberts joined the others at the enlistment office and there struck a snag. He was rejected for physical disability, and instead of going over there, he was sent to one of the shipyards.

For a number of years he owned Planwydd, the resort on Palomar, and there he became known to many San Diegans. Jack has lived in California since 1916, much of the time in San Diego County and city. He is a nephew of Lloyd George, the relationship to the famous British statesman coming on his mother's side of the family tree. Of course, this native son of sturdy little Wales is a naturalized citizen of Uncle Sam, and San Diego is his hometown.

As a sportsman, Jack has played at intruding and sport angling mostly which takes a man into the open camping, living close to nature.

The brochure he prepared to advertise the National Forest Country Club and the architects drawing for the proposed investment remind me of the thwarted dreams that seemed to change our life. The resort association Jack attempted to interest in financing the Country Club became bankrupt and the dream faded—a tattered brochure all that remained. Jack's grand plans for a resort on Palomar failed.

For more than two decades, my heart was heavy with words, sad words, troubled words, and negative words. I chose to keep those words hidden in my heart. Troubled thoughts were there, I simply chose not to put them on paper.

Life in San Diego that began as *easy street* suddenly fell under the dark cloud of The Great Depression and enveloped Jack with his own dark clouds. The Depression must have hit Jack like a sledgehammer, and crushed life as he desired it to be. Soon California real estate was dead along with Jack's dreams of prosperity and owning an impressive home. Now, as I look at my letters saved from that tumultuous time indicating frequent moves during the 1930s, I remember how daunting those changes felt.

Though Jack continued to pursue closing other real estate deals, his dream of developing a first class resort on Palomar evaporated. Hopes of taking us to meet his parents in Wales also seemed lost forever. Devastated by circumstances and his inability to provide for his family, Jack struggled to cope with life.

Catherine was twelve in 1930 when the heaviest impact of the Depression hit us and surely, the financial collapse to our own life influenced her as well. Twelve is an age when a child would understand enough to feel the tension, yet probably not the reasons behind what was happening. I could understand somewhat what was happening in the world. Yet I could neither understand nor help Jack with the void into which he had fallen. Years later, subtle hints of resentment towards her father occasionally surfaced from Catherine but disappeared as rapidly as a fast-moving cloud.

Though my journal was silent for those years of wreckage and change, history books record all the facts that preceded and then followed the Great Depression. The dramatic shift in lifestyle made it seem as though suddenly a tornado transported us into another world, another life.

The history books record that 1926 was the highest standard of living in our nation's history. Wages were up and unemployment hardly a problem. Prosperity reigned. I well remember President-elect Herbert Hoover making a promise in 1928 of "a chicken in every pot, and a car in every garage." So, real estate boomed and life was easy street for that year.

The Black Thursday occurring on October 24th, 1929, began the crash of more than the stock market. For us it was, as for many families, a crash of personal dreams and plans. Within a year, over four million people were jobless. Jobless people don't buy homes, and Jack was still trying to make a living from real estate.

Catherine was sixteen in 1934 and the Great Depression, her father's attitudes, and the death of her grandmother were overwhelming her as well. Roosevelt issued a proclamation that year devaluing the dollar by 40%. I imagine that for Catherine it must have been a roller coaster experience during those years of uncertainty. We bounced from living in large, lovely homes to much smaller abodes. The years following the 1929 stock market crash became increasingly bleak

I saved only a few letters between Alice and myself from those trying times. Letters filled with anguish over the unexpected death and loss of our cherished mother at age seventy-six in 1934, followed only two months later by Hylinda's sudden, and surprising death at forty-nine. Alice and I were devastated. We were trying to arrange help for Hylinda's two children Sarah and Sam. Absalom was searching for work, and I felt we must be there for our niece and nephew. They were only eleven and fourteen. My letters to Alice remind me how difficult those days were for both of us. The letters reveal sorrow and frustration at my inability to do much due to our own financial straits. They also remind me how severe Jack's struggles had become.

Still desiring more children of my own, I gladly took in Sam and Sarah for a short time after Hylinda's death. I had only Catherine. Alice gave birth to her seventh child only twelve weeks before mother died (Cameron was a newborn and Rosalyn a two-year-old). Jack did not agree with my desire for us to take in Sam and Sarah while Absalom searched for work during those most desperate years. I was also extremely distressed over the burial of Hylinda in a pauper's field.

Dear Alice, July 17, 1934

Jack and I talked after Sam and Sarah abed last night. Jack thinks I'd better take them back soon, though I'd much rather keep them longer. Absalom wrote them saying its 110 degrees there now. He said to me when leaving to take them to you instead of home when I bring them up. Received your letter with kind offer to meet you part way. I want very much to see you honey. Also, want to talk things over for Sam and Sarah with you.

It's so good to have your letters. Probably Hylinda would rather have had them brought up without any woman in the house than under Jack's point of view and way of doing things. Anyway, he seems to think I should take them back soon. His idea is that Sam and Sarah should go to a boarding school (as he did). Horrible thought to me! Of course, they must feel like fish out of water here, though in some ways very adaptable and anyway very sweet and dear.

Some things in our environment not so good for nerves and health as well as for point of view for children, too. We've tried to feed them up, not able to give them as much milk as I wanted though. Jack thinks if they are away for too long a visit that their county will stop providing. Jack is very busy, expects more returns before very long. We want to get a home when we can.

It has been a great joy and comfort to have them, and I've felt a pig to be the one to have that consolation right now. Far as I know, they haven't shed any tears here. Sam asked me what disease really killed his mother. I wish you and I could have talked to the doctor. I've found Sarah looking very sad. Sam asked me to hear their prayers at night as Hylinda did, so I have every night. It broke my heart all over again when Jack showed definitely last night he thought we'd better take them up soon. I hadn't felt up to more than day-to-day living and felt vaguely we might have them a long time. Sarah seems to feel they might move anyway. We can be glad Hylinda had such high character compared to her burial in a pauper's field. It is not so important, and we shouldn't feel so humiliated about her burial that way. Sam and Sarah haven't said a word about funeral or burial conditions.

I'm not very well and possibly shouldn't try to have them long anyway, much as I want to. I don't suppose Hylinda's clothes are of much value

to make over for Sarah. Our car is not very dependable for a long trip.
I asked Sam and Sarah if they thought they could get along all right at
home alone with their father and they seemed very confident they would.
I wanted to have them until Sarah gained some more weight and they
avoided more of hot weather. I know it is hotter there at Calimesa than at
Wildomar with you or La Mesa with us.

Could you meet us at Capistrano next Sunday? We'd leave here early
to be there nine a.m. and should start back near noon to have daylight. Our
car is more uncertain than ever. I wonder if your car can travel now? It
would help if you could send us a wire about meeting to Jack's office, 7th
Street San Diego. Jack says a wire only costs about $.25. Or you could
phone me at my neighbor, Mrs. Ben Poloc.

Love, Elsie

Dearest Alice July 23, 1934
I hope you'll not try to have the children long now when you and
Ernest thought it best not. It might be too much for you and yours under
the conditions. I wrote to Absalom as you suggested. If you haven't done
it, why not write him suggesting that if his truck will travel he might call
very soon for Sam and Sara at Wildomar and save you a trip.

Sarah expects to use housedresses and aprons of her mother's. Let
me, not you, help with any making over skirts of hers or any of Hylinda's
clothes for her, as I only have to sew for one child. I am finding comfort
in wearing things of mother's, as if she were closer. Maybe I could make a
blouse, two for Sarah out of old silk dresses of Hylinda's, dyeing, or turning
if need be. I used to marvel at the way you and mother could make over
clothes; but I have found it fun and profitable, and I have been more
successful than I would have imagined myself, in late times. Of course,
I don't want all the pleasure of sewing etc. for Sam and Sarah if you can
manage to do some of it; but I don't want you to feel you must when I
seem the more logical one to do it. Understand? You mustn't do too much.

I thought it easier for you and better all-around to delay our
trip to Wildomar now that Sam and Sarah so enter the problem. Jack
thinks I'm willfully assuming responsibilities not mine. Nevertheless,

if Absalom should go far to work and take them or make some other arrangement involving a great change, or move, that might make much difference. Anything you arrange is okay with me as far as sharing mother's things. You need not stop to ask me. Anyway, I think you should have the most, as I thought before, because of having mother there, practically with you and because Aunt Mamie gave us so many things. Sam and Sarah have wonderful possibilities. Maybe if we wait awhile developments such as moving might help settle problems. I think Sarah hungers for beauty or at least pleasantness and niceness about her. I do think we ought to do what we can to give Sam and Sarah more cultural and ancestral influences.

I talked a lot to Sam and Sarah about old family incidents, etc. and they loved it. I think it helped to make Sarah, at least if not Sam, feel a sense of comfort, or still closely belonging and having for always a family. She seemed eager to hear anything about her mother; and loved to see old pictures of her, etc. I think in some ways Hylinda strongly brought them up in the old family traditions and with a sense of background. I think Sam and Sarah are very affectionate and do feel deeply about their mother.

I warned Sarah not to work too hard and she said Absalom was always telling her that. Still, I dread to have her try to keep house. You may see him soon and maybe can warn him more about her age and thinness. Sam has been at times difficult. If Absalom is not on a job, I think he'd do a lot. If he is, couldn't he get washing done at least, if not a housekeeper? Sarah realizes she's not strong. She has more energy as well as household skill than I'd have expected.

I feel so sorry about the problems of settling mother's estate. I think Absalom would be very amenable and try to help. Let us know if we can do anything.

If it makes you feel too bad to see Sarah in Mother's clothes why not get Beatrice or Dorothy to ask her not to wear them while she is with you. Do take care of yourself, honey; and let the children do things for themselves and each other. Don't keep Sam and Sarah long! That very lovely letter of yours did me much good. Absalom has written to me "I love Sarah and Sam more than my own self. I am risking my life every day for their sake. I hope all are well and I love all of you."

Love to all, Elsie

This letter written to Alice five years later shows how things were continuing to become more difficult.

January 22, 1939
8111 Pasadena Ave., La Mesa

Dear Alice,

It was very good to have your letter come today on my birthday itself. I also appreciated the fact that you wrote me consciously on Mamie's birthday Mrs. Wood made a long call this afternoon. I told them what you said about wondering if anyone in the world was like Aunt Mamie and Mrs. Woods said she wondered that, too. Lila Pollock made me a gorgeous big angel food cake and brought it over beautifully decorated with thick white icing and an old-fashioned nosegay in the center on a lace doily, violets around a deep red perfect and very fragrant rose and on a tray of white covered cardboard with lace doilies and flowers about it.

Catherine was feeling bad because she had nothing for me. I told her she couldn't give me anything I'd appreciate more than getting me the use of Kay's typewriter for a while, as I haven't had one for a very long time. She's been helping Kay with end of the semester work at college, and Kay had left her typewriter. I used it so much, and so did Catherine who has been longing for a chance to practice typing, that Jack surprised us by bringing the machine I'm using now for us. It's an old one he could get cheap, spending hours renovating oiling, etc., so it's fine. We were both thrilled, and honestly glad for once, he had the sense to get something cheap instead of his usual idea of the best or else nothing. I seem to need to get used to the touch of this, though, so far used only on this letter.

The church here has Dr. Roy Campbell as the new pastor. He'd retired from his long and noted service at the first Congregational in San Diego, where we used to sit under him when we lived there. The whole town is very proud of having him come here. He's a Pomona man, and close friend of Alice M. Parker. Catherine still does many church things despite Jack's objections, and I practically never go, much as I'd like to. Maybe I'll do more soon of that sort of thing, anyway.

Catherine is again at the across-the-street neighbors tonight, the Higgins, staying with the children while the parents are away. I think I told you they let her use the phone a lot and she does other things for them. Catherine is in a drama class as well as the Spanish class. We hope she is able to take typing, etc. in classes this coming term, unless she somehow otherwise occupied. She doesn't really want business training, thinks she doesn't like that kind of thing. However, she and I both feel it might be very wise anyway to make a desperate effort to go to business school, since we don't dare count on more college for her, bitter, as it is to think she may not get more. Jack still talks as if she would. She wants to teach, or if not that to do something else of that type that requires college, as that's the kind of thing she does well and is interested in. She may have to do something that requires less training, and I remain extremely anxious for her to go away from home somewhere. I wish we could get her off for a little visit, but so far, we haven't the bus fare. I still hope that someday Jack may be more his old self. He does just these last days seem less excitable, etc. Maybe he really will have money for more education for her someday, if she isn't altogether too old then. She ought to be doing something towards the future now, and certainly wants to. She's been wonderfully brave and good about conditions.

She went to another dance at the Coronado Hotel, a fraternity one, but hasn't lately been out with that crowd, though one of them took her driving the other evening—if that could qualify as going out. She can't afford to keep up with them. Charlie still takes her for a drive or a show once in a while or to league. Catherine has at least one would-be escort she carefully evades. I surely long to give her a normal chance and a normal life. For a long time that has remained quite impossible here at home.

How I'd love to be able to have her cousins here a lot! I had a nice letter from Sarah yesterday. That was a grand letter I had from you earlier. I was as usual ever so thankful for the money order enclosed. I was terribly busy a few days when Kay's typewriter was here, and I didn't know then when I'd ever have a chance at one again.

I think it's lovely for your children to have such a hospitable home. I know you must enjoy ever so much the social times, and all the recent additions and improvements in your furnishings. I'd love to see them and you honey. It is much too long since we've met. Someday! I get hungry to see you. I was glad you told me so much about things. Beatrice surely is the one in her generation with special appeal! I warmly hope her affairs of the heart eventually will work out most happily, and as Aunt Mamie used to say, that she'll know her John Henry. It must keep life interesting for the whole family!

Catherine has been doing a little more altering of clothes for herself. I think she's quite clever at it. I'm afraid this letter sounds depressing. If we can hold on while longer, maybe things will brighten.

> Love to all, especially you my dear sister,
> Elsie

As I look back, I see that many of my poems and articles I wrote during those hard years were about Palomar. My heart and mind still overflowed with dreams of my mountain. Love that began in a sixteen-year-old girl had not diminished with time and distance. I continued writing, even after we sold my typewriter. I wrote in pencil or ink, I wrote on scrap paper but I wrote.

Perhaps the letters I saved explain what I couldn't say. Perhaps the articles I wrote reveal my heart.

Our Friend Nature
by Elsie Roberts—June 1931
Printed in Parent Teacher Courier

A thousand years from now historians are apt to declare the parents of this era a paradox—studying the problems of child training, as they were never studied before, yet too absorbed in their own hectic rush to come too close to their also over-stimulated children. Sometimes this accusation is too true. There is at least one very definite way in which parents and children may not only come to understand each other better but both acquire meanwhile that vital sharing of common interests and joys, sense of leisure and serenity. This is in cultivating the out-of-doors. It need not be done with hoes or tractor, but by being upon more intimate calling terms with nature. Grant that modern life is too complicated and artificial for the greatest good of the coming generation, then go to the direct source for all that is simple and natural.

In California, even city dwellers have abundant opportunities to give their children recreation, if not work, out-of-doors. Yet often we neglect these opportunities. Of course, the youngsters play outside. As they grow older, do they always arrange for picnics and mountain weekends as eagerly as we might? Is a love of the great open spaces an essential part of their lives, and is it fully satisfied? Is a beach or mountain trip included in the budget even if the renovating of the furniture needs to be postponed?

The very recent trend is, fortunately, a reaction back to the land. There is a growing appreciation of the out-of-doors. We have innumerable nature study groups and summer camps for boys and girls, while out in the rural districts the splendid 4-H clubs are becoming more and more popular, helping the farm youngsters to value their peculiar advantages. Some modern parents, no matter how fond of bridge or business realize that hikes to the foothills with their children are more important. One such admits that she hopes they may prove a specific antidote to jazz.

Like all other good things, a real interest in nature needs to be encouraged and developed. A parent can't afford to loaf on this job. The earlier he starts and the more fascinating he makes it, the more surely the child will respond. Diversions particularly strengthen the bond between fathers and mothers and their offspring. As the youngster's energies seem unsatisfied by scenery alone, it is well that books, hobbies, and sports should give added contact with nature, and foster a deep friendship with her.

Yet nature in her various aspects is herself fascinating, even thrilling. Here the outside is always available, and though we do miss the novelty of definitely separate seasons, we find these in our own never-too-distant mountains. Often California families not only stay there in the summer, but also take the children to see the snow in the winter. Yet many do not realize how easily they may also let their native sons and daughters know the charm of Eastern Springtime—that burgeoning of bare boughs, those bursts of clear streams from every mountain slope, those meadows blossoming with butter cups and blue violets and aged with tasseling oaks, and the still white beauty of dogwood trees. Every child has the right to discover for himself that it is anything but boresome to leave the beaten trails, to know the forest primeval.

An appreciation of beauty is indeed the greatest asset of culture. An acquaintance with nature is a vital part of education, interpreting and adding to the enjoyment of the formal arts, while in itself it is indispensable.

A charming girl lately exclaimed over a marvelous thicket of the azaleas beside a far isolated mountain stream, "They smell like heavenly French perfume! But why did anybody plant all those way off here?"

How many, having eyes see not! It is as true as it is trite that one's vision is foreshortened by his limitations, and he sees only that which he knows how to look for. So many a youth, tragically and unnecessarily bored, goes blindly on, never dreaming of the freshness and glory of the out-of-doors. If a primrose by a river's brim is to him nothing more, it is his loss, but perhaps his parent's fault. What better can education do than to train his perceptions and enlarge his capacities?

In this so-called machine age the aesthetic urge needs special encouragement, and with it the inextricable intermingled spiritual values. Nature can add unspeakably to inner resources. Where there is the feeling that a thousand years are but as yesterday, sanity comes out of chaos. The famous surgeon, Dr. Charles Mayo is quoted as recently telling a women's club that the very prevalent mental disorders seem caused by our speed of life and the fact that we are an emotional people. Overwrought nerves are considered one great cause of juvenile delinquency. Though a youth's fiber can weaken by too much excitement and ease, instincts can remain right. As a reaction to the modern strain, he craves the primitive, reveling in Western novels and talkies. Let him know the figurative West in a literal way!

1938—Palomar Mountain Article
Elsie Roberts

There is no more beautiful or fascinating spot—in Southern California, at least—than Palomar Mountain. Its scenic charm lies in both the variety and degree of its beauty. The usual Californian outlook is anything but monotonous; yet the heights of Palomar are still intriguingly different. There are numerous hints of the Eastern states, in contours and streams and vegetation. Here are even the definite seasons that are so intermingled in the country below: the spring of tasseled and pastel-shaded black oaks, blossoming dogwood and meadows of blue violets; a summer when cherries and gooseberries are ripe; an autumn of apples, glorious color, and a crispy tang; in winter when snow falls and long icicles hang from the eaves. Yet the typical Western effect is here, too. Beside the mountain springs are the indescribably lovely azaleas and rare lemon lilies, while scarlet larkspurs and huge lupines splurge vivid color on the crests. Live oaks precede the pines, firs, and hemlocks down the far-flung slopes where steep precipices frame infinite reaches. Ruggedness and delicacy unite with the unique and distinctive appeal.

The unexpected, the picturesque, are everywhere and are dominated by the superb grandeur only mountain peaks can give. Seasoned travelers, recalling the Grand Canyon and the Alps, are awed into silence when they look off from Palomar to the edge of the world. Evergreen forests march down the ridges. Beyond the wild canyons, range after range, are the rolling foothills, softened by fields and orchards and enriched by nestling lakes, their mesas dotted with busy towns. The Pacific lies at the outermost limit, curiously near and clear in the mountain air.

Palomar is a world of its own, with its high valleys sheltered by wooded slopes. There is always some alluring new crest or hollow to investigate, a trout stream to follow, the chance of seeing wild creatures in their haunts. There are good roads for those who choose them; charming trails for the saddle wise; and, most fascinating in this too-sophisticated age, the jungles—the forest primeval. It is no wonder that this was the mecca for campers even when it meant a steady six-hour climb for teams over a dreadful road. Now cars speed up the gradual grades. If fresh scenes and pastures new attract the motorist, he may travel the twenty-mile length of the mountain, largely along its crest, and descend at the other end. It is also nine miles wide, and if he is wise, he will stop by the way and explore some of Palomar's endless delights.

Catherine graduated from high school as the class valedictorian in 1936. She had the same desire I'd had years before to go to college and become a teacher. Even Jack's charm could not help insure financial survival during those hard years. Yet, somehow, by 1936, we managed to save enough money for Catherine to attend my alma mater, Pomona College, for a year. For Catherine a college education became an elusive dream. Eventually she settled for an office job.

By 1938, the U.S census showed maybe as many as ten million were still jobless, almost a decade after the crash of the stock market and its crushing effect on the real estate market. We were also aware that life in Wales for Jack's family became more complex and dangerous. Not long after 1938, Britain declared war on Germany. German bombers were killing thousands in Great Britain. War and financial loss added to the ocean that separated us from Jack's family. The war department censored Jack's letters to his mother. His father had died the same year I lost both my mother and Hylinda. I earned a small income from the articles I was writing during those lean years.

Catherine was twenty-four when she married Charles Beishline in Yuma, Arizona, in 1942. The U.S. Marine Corps drafted Charles and shipped him to Hawaii. Shortly before Catherine married Charles, I resumed my career as an educator working as a school librarian. I know it came as a blow to Jack—for me to become the breadwinner. I was fifty-four. I enjoyed working as a librarian, sharing literature with young, eager minds. I sorrowed over what was happening to Jack.

During those war years of gas rationing and meager income, it became necessary for me to rent one room of a colleague's home in La Mesa so that I could work. Jack took a room in the Saint James Hotel while he attempted to sell real estate. We spent weekends together at Catherine's home on Juniper Street in San Diego when possible. When the war ended in September of 1945, I was still teaching and living in one room of a friend's home. When Jack became too ill to live alone in 1946, he moved in with Catherine; she was expecting her second child. Jack had lost the race with cirrhosis of the liver. On the last day of 1946, a year after the war ended, Jack died. He was not yet fifty-nine.

San Diego Union—January 3, 1947—Obituary—John Planwydd Roberts

Private funeral rite for John Planwydd Roberts fifty-eight, San Diego County resident for twenty-eight years and a nephew of England's World War I Prime Minister the late David Lloyd George, were conducted yesterday in Cyprus View Mortuary chapel.

Mr. Roberts, who died Tuesday, Dec. 31, 1946, in a local hospital, often spoke of his famous uncle whom he had known well when as a boy he visited in North Wales the home of Lloyd George and the mother of the future premier.

In 1904, Mr. Roberts left Wales and went to Alberta Canada, where he was employed by a lumber company. He also homesteaded near Great Slave Lake in Canada. Twenty-eight years ago, he came to San Diego County and he and Mrs. Roberts owned and operated a summer resort on Palomar Mountain for six years. The resort was named Planwydd after Mr. Roberts' middle name. Later, the Roberts moved to San Diego. Mr. Roberts, who in recent years had resided with his wife at 3057 Juniper St., also was a former County real estate operator.

I continued to work as a librarian for the next decade after Jack's death, sharing my love of literature with schoolchildren. Once again, I returned to the dream of spending time on my beloved mountain.

11

Coming Home to My First Love
1947-1987

Autobiography
By Elsie R.H. Roberts

My spirit knew unrest:
Joy vanquished pain, but then
Pain followed Joy again.
I set my spirit on a noble quest,
A steadfast Hope to win—
That hour despair crept in!

And when, all wearied out,
it sought for rest,
Rest was there none,
For Peace was gone,
Peace, more than Joy and
Hope desired the best,
I followed mountain ways,
The lilacs touched my face,

The fern fronds bent in grace
And in the firs, the wind sang ancient lays.
So to the crest I came
Where richest fancies flame,

And beauty holds a pageant all the days.
Down from the peak, one sees

Across the canyon's trees
The hills and plains that reach
The sea's blue haze.
But, lo! O'er it all there lay,
Touched with a mystic light,
The cloud banks, drifted and white,

Exquisite, visible silence
and the snow of May
The distant sea was gone,
The heights and the depths were as one.
In that holy, boundless calm
TO FEEL WAS TO PRAY.
O'ER ALL Nature the vast hush stole,

And it touched my spirit, my soul,
With the Peace of God, that came
At the close of the day

Just as the death of my brother Gilman inspired our family's first trip up Palomar in 1904, the death of Jack carried me back to my beloved mountain in 1947. Once again, I retreated to the lush green trees and fragrant air to soothe my spirit. During the decades away from my mountain, my devotion had not waned. The apple ranch now lingered as a precious memory of early years there.

Milton Bailey's widow, Adalind, had begun to subdivide their land. My daughter Catherine, her husband Charles, and I purchased a small lot there in 1948. We were very happy to buy some lots close to the old Bailey home. I had never known Adalind Bailey well before, but she became a very dear friend. Our grandchildren are the fourth-generation to be friends. She has been a gracious hostess to the many who continued to come to the old place, her beloved "house by the side of the road," the center of the community of cottages where we have our cabin, too.

Catherine's husband, a graphic artist, demonstrated his creative abilities in countless ways. There was no electricity available, so Charles hand cut the lumber that had been milled on the mountain. He built our small cabin as a weekend and summer retreat. There was a room for me, and a room for Catherine and Charles. The Beishline children—Dan (aged five) and baby Barbara—slept in the living room. The Bailey Mutual Water Company provided pure, cold spring water. Charles built a handsome stone fireplace, and a cast iron vintage cookstove provided the means to cook and bake. An actual ice-box kept food cool, and kerosene lanterns offered evening light.

The Beishline family spent almost every weekend at this mountain retreat. I often joined them. My fragile dream was to eventually retire and retreat to this charming but rustic, little cabin on my mountain. I found an old note where I had scribbled:

> There were three phases of my life on Palomar. The first began as a girl when we took that trip in 1904. The second was living there as a wife and young mother in 1918. The third was as an elderly widow with my grandchildren. In the years

between, I dreamed of Palomar and longed for it with great hunger.

Imagine how a woman must feel when her son is elected president of the United States. That is the way I felt when my mountain was chosen to be the site of the world's largest telescope. At last, the world was recognizing its marvelous and unique qualities.

If it is commendable for a citizen to claim the city proudly as his own, is it too outrageous that one should, with passionate devotion, claim a mountain? Every mountain must have its devotees, and Palomar has many.

Beishline and Roberts' cabin

There were indeed rattlesnakes and no doubt still are many. I have seen mountain lions, wild cats, and foxes. Once a bobcat mated with our house cat, producing kittens with tails of different lengths! I suppose many of these same animals still live in the Palomar [Agua Tibia] wilderness area, a large acreage and a part of the mountain where there are no roads or trails, and where people are not supposed to go. California has a number of these wonderful wilderness areas where the natural wilds cannot be disturbed by civilization.

In the spring, the dogwood and blue and white lilacs in Faerie Wood and the Boucher Orchard were spectacular. The blue violets, buttercups and other wildflowers in the meadows were lovely. In August, the fields were white with buckwheat blooms. By early autumn, the ferns started turning a golden brown, and acorns would thud on the roof. Goldenrod and poison oak began to change to a soft rose color.

From my window, I would watch the squirrels with their fluffy tails sitting in the tree just outside. I watched mother birds giving little ones crumbs, a redheaded woodpecker backing down the tree stopping now and then to look over his shoulder at crumbs below, finally leisurely pecking and pecking though the other birds usually swooped and flew off. The wind in the trees sometimes sounded like an ocean roar. The Bible says in the book of Psalms to 'lift up your eyes unto the mountains.' With delight I did that.

I retired from the La Mesa School District in 1952. I then became a resident librarian at the small, private Brown School for Girls in Glendora, near Los Angeles. There I attempted to infuse my love of literature to yet another group of students. I had a room in the girls' dorm. My granddaughter, Barbara, tells me that she vividly remembers trips as a child to visit me there. Her father would loudly call out "Man in the hall!" upon entering the dorm.

As I approached age seventy, I returned to La Mesa, and I savored delightful hours in the company of Catherine and her family. My season of life at this point became a time devoted to my grandchildren, now numbering three with the addition of Nancy in 1951. There were no homemade cookies or home-cooked meals at my house. Instead, I served up family stories and even paid the grandchildren to memorize poetry.

My 1952 letter to Alice, written six years after Jack died, adds insight into changes in my life. At age sixty-four, I was at last building my own little nest. My long-deferred dreams bubbled to life in that letter. I faced compulsory retirement in 1953 from my position as a public school librarian. For

Librarian Elsie Roberts

years, I subsisted in one room of a friend's home. Finally, I saw the dream of owning my own home coming to life.

1952

Dearest Alice,

The years go fast and I have tried not to think what will happen when I can no longer work at the library. The idea was to live at Palomar, but I kept thinking if I had some place around La Mesa, I could possibly continue work of some kind (possibly in a bookshop). I'd be unavailable if all the time in the mountains. Anyway, places to rent are few and high. I had lived with the horrible thought of existing with only kitchen privileges at most, as for eight years and more, I have done.

They passed a regulation for compulsory retirement at age sixty-five. I was looking for a one-bedroom cottage. Catherine and Charles advised me a second bedroom to rent would bring income. I found minimum for La Mesa is 650 sq. foot. So a tiny one was out, anyway. Tonight I finally paid $25 down on a $1,800 lot. Good location, near our new school, near bus line as needed, not too far from stores to walk. We saw a model home similar to one I may have built, two bedrooms, meaning the 650 square feet are provided. You may both think I'm crazy. It should be a very good investment if I found I couldn't keep and needed to sell. Builder would charge $5,175. Tenant (probably a teacher) will rent for about $40 a month. Entire price, including bank charges would be over $7,000. But if I stay this coming year, I should have about $60 a month teacher's annuity as long as I live. With rent of room that would be around $100 and a happy place to live. Builder payment thought might be around $44 a month and little apartments rent for $60 or more generally. Hope I'm not crazy to plan it! Of course, loan might somehow be refused. I'll have around $2,500 cash for a lot and to start the rest.

It gave me a new lease on life to think of having a home, after living for so long in a room I couldn't even arrange as I wanted. Though at first I didn't dream of more than three rooms at most, I've learned so much in the last ten days or so! So now, I'm holding my breath to see if loan does go through. I am known here in La Mesa. That will help me to get tutoring or teachers to board.

Lots of Love, Elsie

I had not driven for years and I enjoyed walking to La Mesa or catching the bus to wherever I wanted to go. My son-in law, Charles, drove me weekly to the grocery store. I no longer cooked or baked bread or pies. Somehow, I maintained my health while eating frozen chicken dinners, yogurt, cornflakes and See's Chocolates! I was able to walk to church and the local library to secure my stack of reading material for the week.

It became my quest to create within my grandchildren a love for reading, as I had loved it. When I would offer to grant the grandchildren a wish for their birthday, they usually requested a bus trip to downtown San Diego to visit used bookstores. We would spend the day exploring them. I would buy them a twice-loved book, and we would have a memorable lunch at Manning's Cafeteria. Barbara tells me she thought it was heaven to walk past those long display cases of prepared food and choose whatever she desired. She always chose the Jell-O cut into small cubes, served in a fluted dish topped with whipped cream. I always chose pie. *Apple pie!*

Occasionally I would announce to the grandchildren that it was time to look in my cedar chest. It held all my treasures and memorabilia. On the bottom the dress my grandmother had worn to an inaugural ball at the White House remained; along with the dress were elaborate invitations to two such balls. One of my mother's satin wedding slippers complete with dried orange blossoms from her bouquet nestled there in my cedar chest as well.

There were letters from a missionary in Burma written in the 1880s, Civil War era letters, as well as all of the Arizona letters and a few others. There were also things that must have seemed strange, like knee buckles from the days when men tightened their knee length pants with buckles, and a piece of George Washington's first coffin. The children seemed to love looking at the vintage papers that the family had bothered to bring from Virginia: a receipt from the purchase of a horse; a document noting that as Justice of the Peace, Alonzo Hayes was paid one dollar for issuing a warrant against a man charged with an affray. There were many fascinating and amusing snippets of life in Virginia.

When I was eighty and Alice was a mere seventy-five (though we were living on meager budgets), we chose to travel together to England and Wales. After all, we had never met any of Jack's or Ernest's families. It was too late to meet the parents of our late husbands, but Alice had a brother and sister-in-law in England. I craved seeing the countryside in Wales and meeting Jack's cousins.

———

So In 1968, we two sisters resolved to go meet the remaining relatives in Great Britain. Alice and I were both known for our pluck. This two-month adventure was the fulfillment of long deferred dreams.

We carefully planned and were delighted with our experience. I was back to recording a journal. Some people described us as spunky little old women, full of zest and joy. We had such a marvelous time that we repeated the trip together again to England when I was eighty-two. Here are excerpts from my journal:

On our second wonderful trip to Great Britain (and I do mean <u>great</u>!) Alice and I left Los Angeles June 18, 1970. This trip lasted for nearly three months and we each paid $280.00 for our flight.

Alice had almost unlimited energy. As I was eighty-two years old, she was determined to take good care of me, which she constantly tried to do. Alice always hunted for the B and B, while I stayed by the goods wherever the taxi, train or bus stopped. Then she'd come back with a cab that took our luggage and us both to the destination. Sometimes it was in a private house with one room available for rent. The price was usually around three dollars each per night. We liked when we actually shared a private home, rather than a so-called guesthouse. We saw far more of the life in Britain and made more real friends than if we had stayed in a huge tourist hotel.

So that Saturday morning, on our arrival at Stansted Airport we were in England once again. Marvelous, incredible as that was, when after the briefest preliminaries we noted a small local bus. A very young driver was just ready to start the otherwise empty local bus.

"Oh, I'm not scheduled to take passengers at this hour," he said. Then he must have noted our concern as we explained that the special bus for London had just pulled out. "But if you want to go to Bishop's Stortfort, get in. That's where I'm going."

We didn't have the very restful chance to catch up on sleep that Alice had so much wanted. However, that young bus driver was not the only person to show us heart-warming kindness and friendliness. There in Great Britain, (from arrival on), the people we met always enriched our stay and gave us great happiness. Meanwhile, as so often, we had adventures and fun.

When on that afternoon we failed to locate a bed and breakfast, we reluctantly made a reservation for overnight at a local pub where we had been told we might be accommodated. We had stayed before at fascinating old inns that were really also pubs, and I, at least, particularly enjoyed the old English atmosphere there about which I had always read. Somehow, this place seemed different, with connotations of an American saloon. Maybe I was subconsciously reminded of the terrifying experience in Jerome, Arizona, on my way to my first teaching job. Now, fifty-seven years later, perhaps the corner pub "Robin Hood" on a rather dreary street reminded me of that earlier experience. Anyway, my dubiousness made me act, I very much fear, a bit like an "ugly American"—the last thing I wanted to be in Britain.

Not far from our hotel, I suddenly noticed that we were in front of the police station, and I made a fool of myself. "I'm going in and ask about that place," I said. Alice sanely hesitated, but in we went, to see several pleasant looking uniformed men talking together.

One of them turned to us. "We are two elderly Americans who haven't found any place to spend the night but a pub called 'The Robin Hood,' I explained. "Would you please tell me if it is perfectly respectable, for us?"

For a second the officer just looked at me. Then he and the other policemen simply howled. At least we were reassured. Maybe "the publican," as a formal Englishman later referred to the bar's owner, was the town's most outstanding citizen. We were assured that the pub was quite all right.

The hotel called a cab to take our luggage and us to the "Robin Hood." And the taxi turned out to be an ordinary car with a girl driver. It was that charming, friendly, most thoughtful girl ("Call me Margo," she said) who carried even farther the helpfulness shown us by the young driver of the bus from the airport. At the pub, we were told that we could leave our baggage, but the room wouldn't be ready for us before 8 o'clock in the evening. We agreed with obvious regret.

"And we were staying here instead of London for the weekend for extra sleep before going on to London," Alice sighed. "My sister needs some rest this afternoon."

"That's no problem," Margo said. "I live several miles out in the country, taking phone calls for jobs from there. You can have the place to yourselves most of the afternoon, and sleep if you like." It was a lovely drive to her attractive home. She settled us in the living room with its davenport and big chair with a footstool, showing us an available bedroom. "Tea first, though," she said, and brought it to us with cookies (biscuits she called them, of course).

She left us there for several hours, returning to say she'd take us back to town now before another appointment. We must stop a moment on our way, though, as her mother wanted very much to meet us. When we paused before another pleasant house set back from the street, her mother came out to the car and greeted us as old friends. "Why, I could've taken you for the night myself, if I'd only known," the mother said. Alien travelers in Britain?

Margo had to hurry on; and as it was still an hour or two before eight, long before dark in June that far North, and an unusually warm and sunny day, she suggested that she'd take us to a park near our pub. Margo left us on a bench with a promise to call for us in time for an early train next morning.

The pub-keeper's wife was almost as smiley as Margo. She took us upstairs to a bedroom that looked as if it were her own, and said that the adjoining sitting and dining room, obviously a private family room, was for our use, too, television and all. Maybe the owners slept on the bar itself after the closing hours! We hated to say goodbye to Margo at the station next morning, now a friend.

It was a forty-mile trip to London. While Alice went off to nearby Sussex Gardens to hunt a room, I sat with our luggage heaped about me and sipped a glass of brown ale. I was in London, really and truly.

In early childhood, I had many times in my Virginia home sat curled up in a big chair in a room with glass fronted bookcases, lost to all about me, fascinated with the England of old books. Forever after, Britain was a world of enchantment. A little later Dickens was my intense delight; then Tennyson and Idylls of the King, with Scott, Robin Hood, the old ballads. Now here was the brown ale, and the indescribable atmosphere was all about me. It was too good to be true (if anything can be too good to be true).

We went to the old village parish church Sunday, and Monday Ernest's brother Harold joined us for lunch and took us to the ancient Exeter Cathedral in that city and then to his home in Newton Abliot for a

Devonshire cream tea. Marfedd Jones, whose mother was a first cousin of Jack's, met us at Bangor and drove us to her lovely home at Holyhead, Anglesey, for lunch and later high tea.

My overwhelming feeling of belonging to the Welsh was not only from a sense of ancestry. And it was also not only the keen interest that my husband had been pure Welsh and had lived hereabouts. As a girl, I had been bewitched by tales of Arthur. Over and over I had read Tennyson's Idylls of the King in those essential adolescent years. In college Alice Parker's tremendous interest in the Celts and their literature greatly influenced me in her class in comparative literature. All this may have been one reason why I fell in love with Jack, the ardent Welsh lover.

Everything seemed memorable—because we were there, hard as it was to believe. We shopped at Oxford Street, because it was near us and not as expensive as Bond Street. We became familiar with Selfridge's huge department store, so different from those at home. Even the ground floor grocery department is elegant, with the head clerk in tails. The elevator (excuse me, the lift) is luxurious—handsome walls, beautifully cushioned seat and all. Incidentally, the deferential "madam" by which I was often addressed seemed almost as unlike America as the constant "Luv" of the guards in buses!

Alice saw a little more of her in-laws than I did. I accomplished extra resting and then wandered about on my own, either purposefully or merely loitering, absorbing atmosphere. What I had was so rich and such a joy that I wonder if it could have meant more to the most tireless and dedicated tourist, to "go abroad" as Fanny and I so vividly imagined we were doing when we were eighth graders.

When we arrived in Guilford, we were met at the proper stop by a handsome, most English-looking gentleman, tall, military bearing, grey mustache, who said, "Alice" and "Elsie" in greeting each of us with a warm kiss. A taxi soon delivered us to his charming home. He is Roy Charters, the husband of Alice's lovely sister-in-law, Dorothy, Ernest's "little sister Dorothy."

But London weather! We had arrived during a "hot spell" which evidently troubled the natives, but delighted me. I almost always wore a heavy coat over my wool knit suit. By the time we arrived at the Charters' home, I was shaking—and the heat had not been turned on by these very English people. With evident remorse (and probably with amazement at these peculiar Americans), they saw instantly that I needed help. On went the heat, my chair was pushed close to that odd contraption so common over there, white corrugated metal panels that I believe carry hot water and to my thinking are quite inadequate. They couldn't have been more hospitable, like all the in-laws we met, my Welsh and Alice's English. Everything so immaculately kept, even the garden! (Do they never say "yard?")

After ten days in London, we went to its suburb, Ealing, to visit another of Alice's sisters-in-law, Grace Thomlin. The day the Queen was opening Parliament we simply had to try to see her on her way. We decided to leave our luggage in a locker at Paddington Station, so that we might go directly to the station after the big event. Cabs had always seemed to be cruising past the hotel, so I waited by the packed baggage outside while Alice went to hail one. Alice tried for an hour while I sat on the suitcases. She finally, after a long stand in line, managed to acquire an empty cab. Though we fairly ran from the nearest stop to where the vast crowds had to gather, we had to stand behind several rows of spectators.

Soon we could see the grand cavalcade approaching. Magnificent guards on their splendid mounts—and finally the carriage, with its gaily-decorated horses. The Queen was so close that if we could have reached through the rows of spectators in front of us, we could almost have touched her. Could it be unpatriotic of a good and loyal American to want so much to see a queen? And yet—I can still remember how long ago as a small child steeped in fairy tales, I used to see that there were classes of beings definitely divided. First, there was God, maybe angels, maybe fairies, then royalty, then people, then animals. So I missed seeing clearly a being that long ago I would have felt was not human. One knows much better now—inhumane, even, some monarchs have been, but still . . . .

We took the train to Edinburgh on the eighth of July. A cab took us to the Angus House Hotel on Queensbury Road. I reveled in that beautiful city. We were near Prince's Street, which I haunted. No wonder it has been called the most beautiful thoroughfare in the world. On one side are shops. On the other side of Prince's Street, are the indescribable Gardens, sloping down to more beauty, and beyond is the high ridge with its impressive stately old buildings, crowned at its steepest, is Edinburgh Castle.

The buses were even more terrifying than in London. Interestingly different from ours in America, especially the double-deckers where the steep, narrow, winding stairway ran up from the wide, open platform. It was the getting on and sometimes getting off that platform that required courage for an old woman whose footing was not quite steady, nor her movements as quick as they used to be. I learned to get in the middle of the line in getting on or off, when possible, and somehow to move faster. Oh, well, when the London guard, of whatever race, invariably addressed me as "luv," or possibly "dear" instead, I was charmed by the sudden realization that I actually was in the land of my dreams.

Alice kept saying I was to do the "brain work" while she did the "foot work" and she left the itinerary to me. Many people we met on our travels must have thought we were two old fools to be roaming about so far from home at our (or my) age, but we were having a marvelous time. Alice insisted on carrying the two suitcases and trying to wrest from me my flight bag as well as holding onto her own.

So, on to the Lake District, a few hours south and then back in England. Beautiful beyond telling! We stayed in lovely Windermere. Every time I stepped from the door of our pleasant guesthouse, I drew a long breath of delight. No American town could have this quaintness of side streets, surely. And all the background beauty, it was Wordsworth country indeed!

It was the eighteenth of July when we reached Windermere, exactly a month from the day we left America. It was very hard to leave this heavenly spot. In dreams, I loiter there.

That was an unforgettable day. Among the hills, clear streams rush down, through lovely woodland. I kept thinking Wordsworth lived here, constantly walking where now we walked. His poetry reflects his deep delight in the beauty here so abundant. Many literary greats lived in this neighborhood, or visited here, besides Wordsworth, his friend Coleridge especially. We saw the home of Beatrix Potter among the hills. Then British Rail again, through beautiful countryside to Holmes Chapel in Cheshire, where Gwyneth met us. She, daughter of Jack's cousin Gwen Ellen, is, of course, Welsh.

Gwyneth insisted on driving us to Chester when we left to take a bus to Wales. Chester was one of the places where Jack went to school. "Rhos" is a tiny village where the old stone houses cluster close together. Now, however, Gwen Ellen lives in a more modern "bungalow." Gwyneth was there too, to drive us all about that part of North Wales, where we were shown the old family home of Jack and his people before him, Playnwydd.

On our first visit, Gwyneth had met us in Bangor. When I looked about at the British Rail station there, wondering if we should have worn red carnations for identification, it was Gwyneth who saw us, two old American women, and came swiftly forward. "Elsie?" she questioned me as I stepped forward; and then her arms were about me. How wonderfully warm they were toward us strange in-laws, all Ernest's and Jack's people!

Auntie Mary, mother of Gwen Ellen, had been sister of Jack's mother, Catherine; they and their brother Eleazer were named Jones. Instantly, I had a sense of belonging. Marfydd took us to see Frongoch, the house in Garn where my mother-in-law Catherine was born to her parents, John and Mary Jones. The houses had and have identifying names, only in large towns and cities having street numbers. In England, too, houses were apt to be known by their names. Jack called our Palomar home and little summer resort Planwydd.

Our last stop was at the graves of Jack's parents, with whom I had corresponded for so many years. They are close to an old church in a neglected graveyard far from Gwen Ellen's home, but where she and Marfydd come faithfully to weed the graves of their people, including those of their "Aunt Catherine," Jack's mother, and of his father, Griffith Roberts. The British are proud of long-lived-in homes. I had said to Gwen Ellen, "Your house is old, isn't it?"

And she had answered, "Oh, not so very old—only about two hundred years."

To a Californian, that answer was a treasure.

Elsie – in front of Jack's childhood home in Wales

There was rain, of course; and of course it was cold, July notwithstanding. Gwen Ellen kept a bright coal fire burning, however. In London, coal burning is no longer permitted, so there was not a brown fog there that Dickens knew so well.

But how I loved Wales! We went for a little walk our last afternoon and I stood and looked across the green fields to the bay and said in my thoughts, "I can't leave Wales. I can't! It is indeed a land of magic."

When my granddaughter, Barbara, was ten, she began to spend the summer on Palomar in the cabin with me. We devoured books. I sometimes read aloud to her, but my favorite times were when she asked me to share from my wealth of family stories.

Each summer I would decorate a small live pine tree beside the cabin. There I would hang a few small ornaments and inexpensive little gifts. Then I would call out "Summer Christmas" and Dan, Nancy and Barbara would rush out to discover small treasures I collected to surprise them. My three grandchildren all inherited my love of the mountain, spending weekends enjoying the same things I loved so many years before. I taught them to recognize the various animals and identify plants by the colors of flowers and types of leaves. They learned to hear and recognize a coyote's howl, the distinctive bird sounds, and the different fragrances of the lilac, the ferns and wildflowers. I watched with delight as they experimented in feeding raccoons from their hands, feeling momentarily their nails as they took the food offerings. Together we roasted chestnuts and made apple cider and chokecherry jam.

During those years that I spent in the cabin, I became reacquainted with Milton Bailey's widow Adalind. As two elderly widows who had experienced similar days of operating resorts decades before, we became the best of friends.

Milton Bailey had married Adalind Shaul in the San Diego Presbyterian Church in 1913. Adalind came up Palomar as a schoolteacher on vacation. She taught school at the Calaveras School located about five

Left—Adalind Bailey; Right—Stephanie Bailey and Barbara Beishline wearing their grandmothers' old dresses to paint signs

miles east of Carlsbad. She had all eight grades in one room, about twelve children. The children were from the Kelly and the Marron families.

Adalind discovered when she married Milton that she had married a hotel. There were about twenty tents all over the hillside, where most of the people slept. Each tent was erected over a wooden frame that sat on a wooden platform. Inside the tent would be two cots, a washstand and a pitcher and bowl. A large dining room sat sixty, where the guests took their meals. That building included a kitchen and a family dining room for the help, the family and the children. The tents were taken down in the fall and stored. An additional building housed the store and the post office.

As Adalind and I recalled stories of our resort years, she recalled one Fourth of July when they had 100 guests and some slept in chairs at night. The guests came by horses, not many cars and very poor roads. The guests usually stayed one or two weeks; sometimes a month, sometimes all summer. Many prominent families from San Diego, the Marstons and the Engles came as guests. The Baileys kept a dozen horses for rent; they also had two to four cows, as well as chickens and pigs.

Milton had bought the mountain stage franchise. The stage left Escondido at six in the morning, stopping at Rincon. There they would eat lunch and then passengers took the mountain stage up Nate Harrison grade, arriving about 8:30 in the evening. This stage had three seats. Adalind recalled that each seat held three passengers. It was a spring wagon with a top on it. About 1914 they changed to automobile stage, traveling from San Diego three times a week for Palomar Mountain. At first, it was an old Pierce-Arrow automobile used as a stage. When it began to get dark, they had to stop and light the acetylene lights. Sometimes the lights wouldn't work when they became plugged up.

Adalind told me that during forest fires the men would come in for coffee and sandwiches all times of the night. And no matter the hour, Adalind would get gasoline for their trucks. One night Milton came in about 10 o'clock. He had been fighting fire for days.

"Now if you women want to see a fire, just get up and dressed and come along with me and I'll show you a fire," he said.

The fire had come almost as far as the summit, and they had stopped it there. The mountain fires had burned as far as the Cleaver place, about a mile from Baileys. Fire once came from the east side as well, flaming across the desert and then climbing the mountain. Wildfires were an ever-present danger on the mountain.

Adalind served as postmistress until 1958. I remember the fascination Stephanie Bailey and my granddaughter, Barbara, had with the vintage cubbyholes that were used to sort the mail for mountain residents. There was a small open space in the wall of these cubbyholes that allowed Adalind to offer a smile and pass the mail to waiting post office patrons. There were no locked boxes and probably few secrets for those who came to collect their mail a couple of times a week.

Years later the mail became a daily delivery, and Wayne and Shirley Thompson kept the post office at the summit. Barbara and Stephanie walked there every day to collect the mail, buy a coke, and borrow books from the tiny library bookcase that served the small community. The settlement remained small. When Barbara was in high school in the early sixties, she challenged a young man to send a letter addressed simply: *Barb—Palomar Mountain, California.* She was confident that she was well-enough known, and I was pleased that Palomar became *her* mountain now, as well as mine. Delightful Shirley Thompson delivered that fun letter to *Barb of Palomar Mountain.*

Just as I had spent time one summer living in the attic of the Baileys' large, three-story lodge, Barbara spent a number of summers in that same wonderful adobe home, built in the 1880s. Stephanie Bailey and Barbara became the best of friends. Adalind Bailey had hired a charming young Mexican man, Luz Lara, to assist her in the upkeep of the property and the running of the campground. He became somewhat of a "nanny" or chaperone for Stephanie and Barbara. My grandson Dan and Stevie Bailey were close in age and became good friends as well. They all (including Nancy) picked apples and made cider with the vintage apple cider press. They discovered the relics of Indian teepees and the worn holes in the granite boulders—metates—where the Indians years ago ground acorns for flour.

The weekend highlights were the family-focused square dances in the old dancehall. The dining room that remained from resort days, still filled with old crockery and remnants of years past, served as their playroom. They bathed in the out-of-doors bathhouse and did laundry in the aging washing machine complete with hand-cranked wringer. Soda fountain syrup dispensers labeled chocolate, strawberry, and vanilla stored in the dance hall fueled their imaginations!

Adalind and I continued to enjoy our friendship when on the mountain. We would "call" on each other and when the visit was ending, we would walk the caller half way back the short distance between the cabin and the adobe Bailey home. Stephanie and Barbara also adopted this practice of walking each other home.

Nancy and Barbara followed their beloved older brother Dan and his friend Stevie Bailey in occasional mischief making. They all had late night scavenger hunts in the decrepit old Bailey barn and snipe hunts. [Snipe hunts took unsuspecting friends on a hunt for a nonexistent animal.] On weekends, they all walked to an unoccupied cabin taking along leftover garbage to feed the raccoons. They would place their offerings on the large porch and wait for the cute little bandit-faced creatures to appear. Hours were spent by the children decorating the vintage dance hall with crepe paper, sweeping the old wooden floor with sawdust each Friday night, as they got ready to dance to the Wabash Cannonball and the Hokey Pokey.

As the grandchildren became teenagers, they participated in weekly baseball games near the Forest Service Fire Station. The games were a mix of oldsters like dear old Gus Weber, joining with youngsters, a few teens, and the guys working summers as seasonal fire fighters. I think Barbara did not care much about baseball, but those handsome young Forest Service guys were of supreme interest. The girls invited the Forest Service young men to the weekend dances at Baileys. The rest is history. As soon as Barbara finished nursing school, she married one of those young, good-looking Forest Service guys. He says he first

Top—Charles Beishline with Carin, Barbara Waite, Catherine, Elsie, Marcia
& Dan Beishline, Dan Waite, Nancy Beishline, Laura and Scott Beishline
Bottom—Alonzo's apple trees—Barbara Beishline Waite

noticed her as she played third base. She says she finally convinced him that she was a good catch.

After Barbara married and moved away, the other two grand-children moved to the mountain. Dan, his wife Marcia, sweet little Laura and her brother, Scott had a home across from the family cabin. Catherine and Charles were then retired and living on the mountain. Eventually, Nancy took a job working with the school camp on the mountain. All of my family, except for Barbara, was living on Palomar. I delighted in their wonderful return to the mountain. My Mountain was now indeed theirs as well.

Epilogue

History can be defined as, "Something that belongs to the past." While *Elsie's Mountain* aptly fits that description, we also recognize how some things have not changed in over 100 years. In many ways, the Palomar Mountain of 2015 remains much as it was in 1904 when Elsie and her family first discovered it.

Today, we all welcome the two excellent roads that provide a much different (and safer) travel experience from what Elsie had in a horse-drawn wagon. Yet the Nate Harrison Grade is still there, periodically maintained now, but perhaps not a great deal better than it was 100 years ago. Those who are faint of heart best experience it in a four-wheel-drive vehicle.

There is less change than one might expect in the development of the mountain. In some way there is less commercialization now than there was in the early 1920s. In those early years, Baileys sold gasoline on Palomar and eventually the Summit sold it. Today, wise travelers will buy their gasoline before starting up the mountain, because it has not been available up there for many years. The only store has a minimal supply of necessities. If you are hungry, you can try Mother's Kitchen at the Summit. The hours of operation are limited. The tiny post office is open Monday through Saturday and has metal, locked mailboxes similar to what you will find in a small town.

The State Park and U. S. Forest Service campgrounds provide an outdoor experience perhaps not too different from 1904. There is a small church that meets on Sundays in the Fire Department. The little school closed a few years ago.

There are no longer resort-type facilities—no traces of Planwydd and Smith and Douglass resorts remain. The Baileys still provide destination event rentals in the replicated old adobe building I stayed in as a child. It was rebuilt after being destroyed by fire. Cozy cabins are available as weekend or vacation rentals. Located on what was once Robert Asher's homestead, the Palomar Christian Conference Center has wonderful facilities for groups.

The California Institute of Technology observatory has been drawing visitors ever since the 200-inch telescope opened in 1948. Astronomers come from all over the world for an opportunity to view and record the heavens above.

Wildfires are still a severe threat to the mountain community, and residents take them seriously. Many of them volunteer at the two fire lookout towers, which provide a close watch on the surrounding forest. There is also a local volunteer fire department, and the U.S. Forest Service maintains a fire station located where it was when I was a girl. Unlike the equipment Jack and Elsie had stored at their resort in the 1920s, both of these facilities have modern fire-fighting equipment

While some of the original apple trees remain, few of the groves are maintained and there is no longer commercial growing of apples on Palomar. In recent years, Friends of Palomar Mountain State Park has assisted the Park in preserving those trees remaining on Park land. They hold an annual apple festival in October. It is a bit like stepping back in time with crafts, vintage costumes, apple sorting equipment, and a working press that provides fresh cider.

Perhaps the most awesome thought about mountain apple history for me is the longevity of the trees planted by my great grandfather in 1904. In the winter, those old trees appear to be ready to be used for firewood. They are twisted and gnarled, revealing years of neglect. But each spring gorgeous young blossoms appear on these aged trees and each fall the apples delight many of us with apple cider, applesauce, and an occasional apple dessert. It is lovely to see how these old trees can still be highly productive. Makes me think about how we oldsters can still be productive!

The appeal of Palomar remains as it was in 1904, the great outdoors, lush and green in the spring and summer, becoming a winter delight when the occasional snows add much-needed moisture. Wild animals are still abundant: deer, turkey, fox, mountain lion, bobcat, squirrels, skunk and raccoon. While clear days are a rarity now, occasionally on a clear day one can still see Santa Catalina Island "twenty-six miles across the sea" more than eighty-five miles from "Inspiration Point" and a mile below the mountaintop.

A few of the settlers from 1904 have descendants that still live or retreat on Palomar. They include Elsie's family, the Mendenhalls, the Baileys, and the Bergmans. Today the Bergman and the Mendenhall families still maintain cattle ranches atop the mountain.

Gus Weber, who came to work for Elsie in 1921, began a friendship with Elsie's family that would span the next sixty-five years. Gus continued to live and work on Palomar. The Mendenhalls and Baileys also remained friends throughout Elsie's life. The Jolly family eventually had ten children, seven boys and three girls.

Elsie lived to be nearly 100 years of age. She retained her Ansel Adams-like memory almost until her last days. Catherine and Charles remained on Palomar until Charles became too ill to be far from medical help. Charles died in 1995 and Catherine died in 2001. Catherine's oldest son, my wonderful brother Dan Beishline, died in 2013. Now his daughter, Laura along with Dan's grandchildren nurtures a love of Elsie's mountain. My sister Nancy and I continue to enjoy Elsie's mountain. The four Waite children and five grandchildren are developing a heart for life a mile high.

Alice lived to be ninety-five years old. There are twenty grandchildren for Alice, and her great-grandchildren number forty-four. Hylinda's grandchildren numbered twenty as well, with thirteen great–grandchildren and five great-great grands.

Last year several of Hylinda's and Alice's granddaughters joined me on Palomar and we had a lovely time, sharing stories on Elsie's mountain.

Elsie had nine nephews and nieces, and as a child, I never quite understood her special care and devotion for Sam and Sarah. Only after reading the letters and thinking through the puzzle pieces, did I understand my grandmother's desire to help fill the absence of Hylinda in their lives.

She consistently displayed irrepressible optimism. In all of her nearly 100 years of life, I can't recall a single negative remark by her about anyone. The biblical proverb, "In her tongue was the law of kindness," described her perfectly.

Elsie had an infectious giggle and displayed an amazing zest for life. She was a master storyteller. I now know there were stories she purposely never told. Years that perhaps she did not want to remember. I never recall hints of bitterness or anger about the *lost years*, though. Instead, she kept silent about them. I do know that Palomar remained a constant source of joyful memories.

Catherine (my mother) did not speak much about her father except to indicate that Jack sought relief from his own personal depression in alcohol during those difficult years. Since I had no personal memories of my grandfather, Jack, I asked Elsie's niece Dorothy (she was then ninety-eight years of age) to describe my grandfather for me. Of course, she saw him from the viewpoint of a young teenager in the late 1920s. She described him as "charming and generous." Dorothy recalled that when Alice and her family visited Elsie and Jack, they were treated to restaurant dinners by her charismatic uncle.

Elsie's letters also demonstrate the grace she extended to my grandfather, Jack, as she chose not to place blame. She had taken vows on Christmas day 1916, "… from this day forward, for better, for worse, for richer, for poorer, in sickness and in health, until death do us part." I never thought of my gentle, frail grandmother as *strong*. I was wrong. Her strength was not visibly evident; it was a resident strength that sustained and prevailed, and was demonstrated by her serenity and silence in the midst of great trials.

I visited Elsie frequently in her unpretentious home where she spent her last thirty years accomplishing what she adored—writing and reading. As a child, I delighted in her lighthearted tales, even if she chose not to tell the *entire* story. When I think of Jack now, I see him through

Elsie's eyes. She taught me that focus matters much in a marriage. She chose not to focus on disappointments and regrets. I will never forget her priceless recollections and the lessons she chose to teach.

It is hard to imagine a grandmother that could have topped "our Grammy Elsie." She could make the simplest of events memorable. I cannot recall her ever speaking harshly or being without a sparkling smile and a ready giggle—more like a deep chuckle. Nurturing our love of the mountain and all creation was her goal. Each of her grand-children, great grandchildren, and now many of her great-great grand-children continue to be fascinated by her cherished mountain. All she had to share with us was her own self, and she did that with abandon. Grammy's winsome ways, her wonderment at all of God's creation, and her inherent ability to unveil our eyes to see what most pass by—that was our inheritance.

Now Elsie's great-great-grandchildren occasionally come up Elsie's mountain to pick apples from the trees that their great-great-great-grandfather planted in 1904. They come to continue the love affair that Elsie started over 110 years ago. The apple trees planted and cared for by Alonzo, and then Jack, continue to produce an abundant apple crop. The generous owners of those orchards sometimes allow me the privilege of picking apples from those aging trees. There under the trees that Alonzo planted more than a century before, the captivating tales Elsie shared flood my memory. I can picture my mother, as a toddler, running beneath the trees taking one bite of an apple, discarding it and running to the next tree to repeat her taste test while Elsie picked apples. I think if we could be silent for a moment, we just might hear Elsie whispering through the gnarled old apple trees repeating her trea-sured tales: tales of daily life long ago and of enchantment on *Elsie's Mountain*.

Palomar Mountain

Palomar Mountain, located in Southern California in the northern part of San Diego County, is not a single mountain, but a range with several wings separated by high valleys. Approximately thirty-five miles from the Pacific coast, it spans an area roughly twenty miles long and ten miles wide. The landscape varies from grass, chaparral and oak-covered slopes at lower elevations to fern meadows and pine, fir and cedar timber at higher elevations. The mountain at its highest reaches 6140 ft. (1870 m). Palomar was an important hunting and camping ground for the nearby Luiseño Indian bands. White settlers reached the mountain in the mid-1800s and by the turn of the century Palomar was home to small farms, cattle ranches, and apple orchards.

The mountain has known several names. The original Spanish explorers called it "Palomar" (dovecote) for the large flocks of wild pigeons. The Luiseño Indians simply referred to it as "paauw" (mountain). As the mountain was settled in the late 1800s it came to be called Smith Mountain, after Joseph Smith, a rancher, and is so noted on county maps of the period. In 1901, residents successfully petitioned the Division of Geographic names in Washington, D. C. to change the official name to Palomar Mountain. Mail to residents was often addressed to them at Nellie, California. This was never a location or community, rather the official name of the mountain post office, having its origin in Nellie McQueen, the first postmistress. The Nellie Post Office moved around and was usually at the residence of the then-current Postmaster. In the days of Elsie's apple ranch and resort, there were only scattered ranches and homes, no town.

Today, most of the mountain lies within the boundaries of the Cleveland National Forest, Palomar Mountain State Park, Agua Tibia Wilderness, and the Pala, Pauma and La Jolla Indian reservations. The 2000 census listed 225 persons as mountain residents.

Glossary

Butterfly farm—Esther Hewlett collected and raised butterflies and moths for sale.

Cars—Elsie used this term when referring to train cars.

Chivaree—Custom in which the community gave a noisy, discordant mock serenade, also pounding on pots and pans, at the home of newlyweds.

Christian Endeavor—The forerunner to modern day youth ministry.

Conscription—Compulsory enlistment for service, typically into the armed forces.

Harrowing—Use of agricultural implement with spike-like teeth or upright disks, drawn chiefly over plowed land to level it, break up clods, root up weeds, etc.

Infantile paralysis—An old term for poliomyelitis (polio).

Iron Water—Iron spring water was thought to be tonic and restorative, increasing appetite and improving digestion as well as other physical improvements.

Machines—Elsie referred to early automobiles as machines.

Marceled hair—Styling technique in which hot curling tongs are used to induce a curl into the hair. Its appearance was similar to a finger wave.

Miscreant—A person who behaves badly.

Mother Hubbard dress—A long, wide, loose-fitting gown with long sleeves and a high neck.

Normal school—A school or college for the training of teachers.

Ram—Water pump that requires no outside source of power other than the kinetic energy of flowing water.

Slackers—A person who evades military service.

Snuggery—Someone's private room or den.

Weir—A stone dam with gauging station built to measure the flow of water, still standing in Palomar Mountain State Park.

Who's Who?

Elsie Hayes Roberts

Jack Roberts

California Family

Alonzo Hayes	Elsie's father
May Carrie Reed Hayes	Elsie's mother
Alice and Ernest Burley Dorothy, Beatrice	Elsie's sister, brother-in-law Their children
Hylinda and Absalom Urshan Sarah, Sam	Elsie's sister, brother-in-law Their children
Gilman Hayes	Elsie's brother
Mary Hale Hayes (Aunt Mamie)	Alonzo's sister
Catherine Roberts	Elsie's daughter—Married Charles Beishline; Children—Daniel Hale, Nancy Lee, Barbara Anne

Virginia Family

Annie M. Hayes (Aunt Annie)	Alonzo's sister
William Nairn Reed	May Carrie's father, Elsie's grandfather
Malvina Amanda Hayes (Grammie)	Alonzo's mother, Elsie's grandmother
Amelia Hanford Reed	William's second wife, Elsie's step-grandmother
Sadie Hayes, George Reed	Cousins

Family Friends

Alice Parker	Harnett family
Fanny Hand	Dr. & Mrs. Shank

Mountain Characters

Nathan Harrison (Uncle Nate)	George Doane
Clark Cleaver	George Mendenhall
Gus Weber	Milton Bailey (later his wife Adalind)
Harry and Alice Hill	Louie Salmons (Hodgie Bailey)
Maria & Lizzie Frazier	Mr. Winbert Fink
Hewlett family	Mr. & Mrs. Stanley Davis
William Bougher	His home & orchard became misspelled as "Boucher"

Others

Hewlett family	Daughter Esther—postmistress & butterfly girl
Mr. Jolly	Mail carrier from Valley Center
Mrs. Wood (daughter Ann)	Worked in San Diego for Elsie
Catherine & Griffith Roberts	Welsh grandparents (Nain & Taid)

Acknowledgments

I thank the Lord for my family and for the opportunity to enjoy Elsie's mountain as a girl. My mother, father, sister Nancy, brother Dan and I have all loved Palomar. Elsie gave me a love of storytelling and encouraged my writing. To be Elsie's granddaughter is an inheritance beyond measure.

I am grateful for readers of *Elsie—Adventures of an Arizona Schoolteacher 1913-1916* who cheered me on to tell the rest of Elsie's story. It has been a delightful experience to meet readers in different states and share stories of family history. Speaking to book clubs, historical societies and interviewing for writers' blogs were icing on the cake.

I could never have accomplished all this without an amazing team of family and friends. My husband Curt has gone over the manuscript time after time helping with rewrites. Our son Dan assisted again with improving the appearance of aged photos. Our daughter Carin Roylance added valuable input to the revisions. My sister Nancy helped me gather photos and letters without which the book would not have been possible. My niece Laura loaned me my mother's baby book and shared photos from 1918-1924. Her mother Marcia Beishline helped with gleaning the right words to describe Elsie.

Janet Shay was my strong right arm, offering encouragement and advice over the last several years. The book would not have happened without her. Sheryl Garza and Eileen Mitchell generously helped with advice. Sheryl advised telling the story as a narrative. The women in the San Diego Christian Writers Guild were helpful with revision ideas. Karen Meyer has been an answer to prayer as a creative editor. She worked with speed and efficiency. Karen lives in Ohio, and has written five historical novels for children.

Peter Brueggeman is a research librarian with a love of Palomar and history. Peter edited Robert Asher's writings. Asher's interesting story is available as on-line research: http://www.peterbrueggeman.com/palomarhistory/AsherMyPalomar.pdf. Peter was a whiz at finding old newspaper articles about Elsie and Jack's years on the mountain. He connected the dots and found those missing puzzle pieces. Lynda Ruth was my typist for a number of chapters. I remain a two-finger typist. Diane King is a cover-design artist extraordinaire. Her covers sell books.

The librarians at the Long Beach Public Library and San Diego City Library assisted me in gathering information and background. The San Diego History Center served as a helpful resource. I appreciated the folks at the Valley Center Historical Society allowing me access to some records there. The New Orleans Public Library supplied a wonderful train photo.

One unexpected blessing was making the acquaintance of Mark Morrison Johnston. Mark and I share William Nairn Reed as a great-great grandfather, but we had neither met nor did we even know of each other.

I had been diligently searching for a photo of Elsie on horseback taken at Mission San Juan Capistrano. She mentioned the photo in her memoirs, and Nancy and I had searched everywhere for it to no avail. It just was not among all the treasured photos we had from Elsie. In the meantime, I posted a photo of William Nairn Reed on an ancestry website. Mark happened to be browsing the site, saw the photo, and contacted me to see why I would have posted a picture of his ancestor. We made the connection and began to share photos. Elsie had kept in contact with her Virginia cousins and they traded snapshots. I sent a number of these photos, of Mark's relatives, to him and he reciprocated with photos from an envelope of his grandmother's marked "California Cousins." I restrained the shout that nearly escaped me (while sitting in a quiet library) when I realized Mark had emailed me the very photo I had been searching for—Elsie on horseback at Capistrano Mission! That photo is included on the cover of *Elsie's Mountain*.

My website: www.BarbaraAnneWaite.com will continue to have tidbits added, along with extra vintage photos that did not make it into the book. I am a research addict, and I regularly indulge in that addiction by sharing historical gleanings that excite me. You can sign up on the website to receive monthly updates. I wrote about Elsie's Arizona adventure in detail in the first book, *Elsie—Adventures of an Arizona Schoolteacher 1913-1916.*

I hope many of you are recording or writing your life events for your children and grandchildren. When I speak to groups, I urge them to buy an inexpensive notebook for each grandchild and leave them their story.

Thank you for reading *Elsie's Mountain.* If you enjoyed her story, I would be greatly encouraged by a short review on Amazon. Writing a couple of sentences can be compared to an extremely generous tip for a meal you enjoyed. It has been my joy to share Elsie with each of you. Treasure your family and drop by for a visit. I just might be on "Elsie's Mountain."

Made in the USA
Coppell, TX
02 May 2020